VISION the

Thank you, & may God bless you
Barbara Wilkes

BARBARA WILKES

VISION *the*

THAT TURNED VALLEYS INTO MOUNTAIN TOPS

TATE PUBLISHING
AND ENTERPRISES, LLC

The Vision
Copyright © 2014 by Barbara Wilkes. All rights reserved.

No part of this publication may be reproduced, stored in a retrieval system or transmitted in any way by any means, electronic, mechanical, photocopy, recording or otherwise without the prior permission of the author except as provided by USA copyright law.

All scripture quotations, unless otherwise indicated, are taken from the *Holy Bible, New International Version*®, NIV®. Copyright ©1973, 1978, 1984 by Biblica, Inc.™ Used by permission of Zondervan. All rights reserved worldwide.

The opinions expressed by the author are not necessarily those of Tate Publishing, LLC.

Published by Tate Publishing & Enterprises, LLC
127 E. Trade Center Terrace | Mustang, Oklahoma 73064 USA
1.888.361.9473 | www.tatepublishing.com

Tate Publishing is committed to excellence in the publishing industry. The company reflects the philosophy established by the founders, based on Psalm 68:11,
"The Lord gave the word and great was the company of those who published it."

Book design copyright © 2014 by Tate Publishing, LLC. All rights reserved.
Cover design by Junriel Boquecosa
Interior design by Mary Jean Archival

Published in the United States of America

ISBN: 978-1-63268-231-4
Religion / General
14.05.20

Acknowledgment

When it comes to acknowledgments and saying thank you to everyone who helped to bring about this book, I have to give God first honors. *The Vision*, my understanding of it and my coming out of the valley, was all made possible because of him. Without his presence in my life I would not have been able to do all that has been done, neither would have the book been written. So I say thank you, Jesus, for being my Lord and Shepherd and for allowing me the privilege of sharing in the vision.

    I want to thank all the people of Belview Baptist Church because they had a part as well. It was during the time I spent with my church family and under the teaching of my pastor and his wife, Bro. Tom and Sue Branch, that I learned the most. From their example, I learned how God expected me to treat others. I learned how to show my love for the Lord by watching them show God's love by helping others who were in need. But most importantly, I heard, studied, and learned about God's word in the Bible and begin to understand what it is saying to all of us. This helped me to understand the vision, and that is what helped me to come out of the valley.

The past several years have not been that easy for all my family and friends. They are the ones who have had to deal with my mood swings and attitudes as God was doing his work in me. They could not escape all the talking I was doing about God as he was trying to help me understand it. But they were patient, understanding, and loving through it all, especially my husband, Fred; my daughter, Melissa; my sister, Becky; and my dear friend Toni. To all of you, I say thank you, and I want you to know that I love you very much.

Contents

Introduction 9
My Journey Begins 11
Getting Acquainted with My Lord 33
His Will 47
Going Back to School 59
The Vision Returns 81
A Time to Celebrate 93
Turning the Curve 103
Retuning to the Valley 133
Paying It forward 157
About the Author 183

Introduction

The book *The Vision* was inspired because of what some may say was a divine encounter with Christ. It's about how Jesus took my hand and led me on a journey of transformation. And even though the road I saw was straight and narrow, there have been a lot of pit stops along the way. In some, I experienced joy while others were hard and full of sadness. But all had a lesson I needed to learn. I believe that we all have a journey to travel in this lifetime. And the choices we make along the way will determine how long it takes us, and in the end our destiny.

I spent the first forty-one years of my life learning the ways of the world and living accordingly. But in the last ten years, I have had a new teacher. His name is Jesus. He has been more than just a teacher. He has been my helper, my protector, my healer, my provider... The list could go on and on. But most importantly, he has been my closest friend.

My Journey Begins

Before I begin to share my journey and how God used the vision in my life, I feel it is important to share a few revelations God has helped me see along the way. It is these revelations that helped me understand why and how I ended up in the valley, and why I was not able to come out of it on my own. But I also believe that it may set the stage and will hopefully bring understanding of why things had to happen as they did in my life.

I begin with the revelation about time and why it is so important for us to be willing to wait when God is saying to us no not yet. It was during one of our ladies' Bible study classes that God helped me see a very important fact, and that is, time is not our enemy; in fact, it can be very beneficial to us. He showed us that the things we read in the Scriptures did not all happen one right after another. But in fact there was a lot of time that passed in between each event, and there were things that did happen in the lives of the people that are not recorded. Because in many cases, it took weeks, months, and even years to get to the places they went to, just so that they could do what God called them to do. As I begin to meditate on this, I was able to see that many times in the beginning as I read God's Word, I did not take into consideration the time it took to get from one place to another. Nor did I consider the things that must have happened in the lives of the people during that time that is not recorded in the Bible. And I will say that there were times when I did assume that God was doing one miraculous thing after another. And I was left wondering why it is that I am not seeing him do things that quickly in mine. But then God helped me see through my own experiences that it was during those times and events that was not recorded that he was able to help those people to grow spiritually and teach them how and what he wanted done. And these things that we read about today in the Bible are there to benefit and help everyone. In the Scriptures, God tells each one of us to wait upon the Lord and be patient and don't give up. And the reason is because just as he ministered and taught the people of the Bible, he wants to minister and teach us, so his will for us will be done. He does that with time and the things we will experience. So in the end, we will know just how much he loves us and all that he can do, but also so he can use us to minister and help others as well.

With the events that happened in my life, God was able to help me have many revelations, which brought understanding of things I had struggled with for so many years. And this brought healing, hope, and encouragement back into my life. But he was also able to help me understand the vision, and why he showed it to me and why it was so important for me to share it with others. Without all of this happening first, I would not have been able to write the book that he wanted me to write. It was during my time of waiting that I gained the most wisdom and knowledge about him because I drew closer to him. I learned how to have faith and trust in him because it was during those times I saw his faithfulness to do what he says he will do and all that I couldn't. I believe the clearer things become, that is when we find the confidence that is needed to believe in God and in ourselves so that we can do what it is he wants us to do. All of this leads us to wanting to obey God, which not only brings blessings into our life but in the lives of others we may encounter.

    I, like most people, have always desired or wanted to have a life on the mountaintop. But I never seemed to know what to do or what roads to take to get me there. There were times in my life when I thought I did, but would always find myself right back in the valley. So as I begin to read the Bible and read the scriptures where Jesus referred to the people as sheep that wandered aimlessly about, I could relate. A lot of times I had felt as though I was spinning my wheels but never going anywhere. I have come to understand that the reason I was so motivated to have this life on the mountaintop was because of God, who represents all that is good, and he created me in his image to be like him. He is the one who put that desire within me to want what is good, because that is his will for all of us.

But unfortunately, we live where there is good and bad. And for that reason, I believe we will or have all encountered a valley or two. Most valleys we experience we are able to come out of eventually because those are what I refer to as the physical valleys. They consist of experiences such as financial lack, loss of job, and divorce, etc. But whenever we come out, we always manage to come out with a little bit of its dirt on us. And if we are not careful, it is that dirt that begins to pile up that can make us feel as if we are in a deeper and darker valley than before. The deeper you fall into this particular type of valley, the sooner you begin to feel as though you are trapped with no way out, becoming like a prisoner within yourself. Through my experiences, I have learned that the only key that will unlock the prison door that we create and allow us to be released is the answers and understanding of all the questions that life sometimes causes. This is the type of valley that I had found myself in.

But because of what I have seen Jesus do in my life and the understanding he has given me, I now know that we find ourselves in this place because we don't know how to let go of things. I guess you could say that we all have a little hoarder living inside of us. Granting, in some people, it is more evident than others. But I think we all tend to hold on to things, both material and otherwise. And once we take possession of something, it is really hard for us to let it go. The material things we store in our closets, our garages, and under our beds.

The Vision

And when they become too much and take over our space, we are able to illuminate the problem by cleaning our house. But the things we store in our minds are not so easy to get rid of. Especially when they are something that we have seen, heard, or experienced and caused hurt.

At the time God showed me the vision, he also put a strong desire within to share it with others and write about it in a book. He has led me to believe that the reason is because there are a lot of hurting people in this world, people who are just like I was. And because they have been hurt, a lot of them are now carrying around the dirt from their previous valleys. And this dirt is made up of unforgivingness, anger, low self-esteem and self-worth, and most importantly the feeling of not being loved. But my hope is, by using my testimony in this book, he can now give others hope and show that there is a way out of those valleys. That even though we continue to live in this world, the world that David refers to in Psalms 23 as the valley of the shadow of death, we can experience and have a life on the mountaintop. Experiencing the peace, joy, and happiness that life has to offer.

Many times over the years, I tried to write the book that God had put a desire within me to write, but the words just didn't seem to be there. And when the time finally came, I was excited but a little scared. I had not done anything like this before and had no knowledge or experience in this field. But I knew my pastor, Tom Branch, did, so I went to him for advice. After we had talked for a while, I left his office with a sense of direction. But there is one thing that he said in our conversation that just seemed to stay with me, and that was, "The valleys we experience in our life are like mountaintops to God."

After much thought and prayer asking God to show me what this had to do with the vision and the book, I found myself sitting at my kitchen table with pen and paper in hand, and I began to reflect back on my life, remembering all the things that I had seen, heard, and experienced that could have caused me to feel as though I was in the valley. And I began to see just how true that statement my pastor had made was.

We all like it when we are on the mountain, because it represents a life where everything is going right for us. But we tend to forget about God, the one who created the mountain and all that can be found there and the one who created us. But when we are in the valleys and the storms of life are overtaking us, the very first thing we do is cry out to him for help. He becomes important to us again. I think for most of us, we begin to spend more time in prayer. Some may even pick up the Bible to read God's Word looking for answers. And for some, we may even begin to attend church, depending on how bad our situation is. It is during those difficult times that we are able to see that we cannot always fix our problems, and just how much we are in need of God's help. And we begin to acknowledge him for who he is, and are willing to take time out of our busy schedule to spend time with him. And I believe that's all God really wants from any of us. Therefore, it only makes sense that our valleys would be God's mountaintops if

THE VISION

that is the only time we are willing to acknowledge or spend time with him. Shortly after I begin this journey, I heard someone say, "That before we can understand where we are going, we first have to understand where it is we have been." That is why I believe reflecting back on our life is so important. Normally it is not until we have come out of a storm that we are able to see things we were not able to see before. It wasn't until I began reflecting back on my life that I was able to see that I was one of those people who took advantage of God. The only time I thought about him was when I was in need of his help. And once my problem was solved, I went about my business as usual, forgetting he even existed. Until the next one arose. Then I called upon him again, expecting him to come, and would get angry when he didn't do what I wanted. Based on how I would feel if someone I really cared about took advantage of me in this way, I began the process of understanding why God did not always come to my rescue in the years past and allowed me to experience some of the things that I went through. Because of his love for me, he was trying to teach me something that I needed to learn so I could have the life that I wanted and he wanted for me. And I needed to see that I needed him to have it. But up until I gained this understanding, I continued to ask God questions all beginning with *why, how, what,* and *when*.

While I was preparing to write this book, I found myself asking the question "What is the spirit exactly?" I had heard my pastor talk about the spirit and read about it in the Bible but never took the time to really understand exactly what it was or what role it played in my life. When I finally looked up the definition in the *Webster's* dictionary, I found that one of the definitions was, "The spirit is the mind, the control center for the whole being." Again after spending a lot of time meditating and praying about this, I began to realize that I had never put a name to the valley I was in, so I was blaming everyone and everything for being there. But then I begin to see that I had been in a spiritual valley from a very young age, because the battles I was fighting were not of the physical kind. My body had healed from the physical hurts, and this allowed me to move on in the physical sense. But the dirt from the physical valleys had now caused a battle to go on in my mind that I could not escape from. I think out of all the valleys we may fall into, these can be the most dangerous and can be the most destructive. The reason why I say that is because they affect our hearts. The things we have stored in our minds go wherever we go and tend to stay with us forever. And over time, as those things pile up, they begin to control how we think, feel, and act toward ourselves and others, and our hearts become hardened and can cause us to lose the key ingredient we need to live a life on the mountaintop, and that is the ability to love and the feeling of being loved. There is an old saying, "You are nobody, until someone loves you." Without love, we lose our sense of belonging, self-worth, respect for ourselves and others, and the ability to have compassion toward anyone else that is hurting. With a heart that has become hardened, then we see ourselves becoming selfish and self-centered. This leads

The Vision

us to where we lose the ability to trust anyone including God. I know all this is true because that is the person I had become and because that was the person I had become, and I was no longer the person that God created me to be. I lived in a spiritual valley for over forty years, and it almost destroyed me and everything that was important to me.

I now see that God had to show me all these things because they are all part of the problem that causes us to feel as though we are in the valleys. And if we do not understand how and why we experience the valleys, we cannot begin to come out, and neither will we own up to the sin in us and see why we are in need of a savior. He has also helped me to understand another reason why we experience the valleys because he helped me see that even though he created us to be different, and the roads he has chosen for us to travel will be different—meaning the places we live, the people we will encounter, and the things we will do. Our feelings and emotions are similar if not the same, and we all live in this world where the Bible tells us in John 10:10, there is one who comes to steal, kill, and destroy us, and that is Satan. It is through our feelings and emotions that he gains control over us so that he can accomplish his purpose. And he will use whatever means that is available to gain that control and attack us where we are most vulnerable. For me he would use sexual abuse to start the domino effect.

I was born on October 21, 1956, and God had placed me in the hands of parents who were Christians. They grew up going to church, and they would continue to go even after they got married, and took me along with them once I was born. It wasn't until I began to reflect back on my life that I began to see more clearly that God was working through them so he could fulfill a plan he had for me. Because as I begin to remember my time as a little girl, I also remembered the times my mother had told me that a week after bringing me home from the hospital she took me to church and gave me back to God. She said that she knew as long as I was in God's hands, no matter what happened in my life, I would be okay. No one knew what my life would consist of, but I believe that God knew. And that is why he placed me in my mother's arms, which turned around and placed me back in his. And before we stopped attending church, I was saved and baptized, and Jesus became my Savior.

But that did not stop Satan from trying to steal, kill, and destroy me or working in my father to begin the process, because at the age of four my life become a nightmare that I could not seem to wake up from. This is when my dad began to molest me and continued for the next seven years. At the age of nine or ten, I was also raped by another family member. By the time I was old enough to begin dating, the very first date I went out on ended with me fighting off the boy I was with. I truly believe that it would have ended in a date rape, because that is what he told me he was going to do. But because my life up to this point had made me feel as though I was put here to be someone's sex tool, after what seemed like hours of fighting, I gave up and told him to do whatever and get it over with; he wasn't the first to do it. It was this response to his attack that I had that shocked him so much that it stopped him in his tracks, and he ended up just taking me home. But this experience left me feeling crushed inside. You could say it was the straw that broke the camel's back, because not only did it throw me back into the valley I had been working so hard to come out of, but I think I fell deeper and harder than before because I saw how it confirmed what it was I was thinking, and that was that no one could be trusted. I had been seeing this person for nearly two years before we ever went out on a date, and I saw myself beginning to trust and hope again. But what took years to build was all destroyed that night by what had just happened, and I remember going back to my grandparents' house where we were staying for the weekend. I went into the bathroom crying. Before long I found myself taking a large bottle of aspirin out of the medicine cabinet, and before I realized it, I had taken every pill that was in it. I just wanted the hurting to stop. With every sexual encounter, it was like someone was pouring salt on my wombs. But this attempt failed because almost immediately after taking the last pill I began to throw up, and it did not stop until they were all out of my system. I was left crying and staring at someone in the mirror that I didn't like and asking God why he was allowing this to happen to me. After what seemed like a very long time, I washed my face and went off to bed. And I got up the next morning going back to pretending that nothing had ever happened. I now see that the moment the sexual abuse started is when I lost the key ingredient I needed to live. Not only did the abuse rob me of my childhood and begin to make me feel worthless, but it took away from me the feeling of love, which represents, identity, security and sense of belonging, ECT. This is when I set out on a journey searching for what I had lost. All the while, I began to live a life full of lies, guilt, and shame, and pretending that everything was okay.

I wasn't able to tell anyone about the abuse when it began because of the fear my dad had created in me from what he was constantly saying to me. He would always tell me after each encounter we had that if my mother found out she would be angry with us, she wouldn't love us anymore, and we would have to leave and may never see her again. I felt like I had already lost my father and his love because of the abuse, and being a child, it scared me to think that I was going to lose the love of my mother as well. So I did as he said and kept quiet, dealing with things on my own. After about seven years, my mother did find out about the abuse, and I began to see that what my dad had been telling me for so many years was a lie. Because even though my mother was angry with my dad, she wasn't angry with me; she still loved me.

My mother divorced my dad when the abuse became known and took my little brother, sister, and me and started a new life. And she would eventually remarry. But by this time, I was seeing the effects that my childhood events had on me. The older I got, the more I could feel myself turning into a cold, lonely, hard-hearted person, leaving me with the inability to trust anyone. Inside I still wanted to love and be loved, but now the fear of getting hurt would not allow me to be who I wanted to be. It was almost like I was living a life of pretense. And this person I was becoming continued to haunt me every day. It just seemed to get worse even after I got married and started my own family. Because I now had new fears and worries I had to deal with as well. Each day I would try to make myself believe that today was going to be better than yesterday, just so I could function and get through the days. And I got real good at suppressing everything down inside, so I thought. There was even times when I thought the memories of my past couldn't hurt me any longer. And those are what I called the good times. But every time I would get to that place in life, something would happen, and the old memories would come back stronger than ever with new ones being piled in on top.

When I was twenty-seven years old, I was in one of those good places. I was happily married, and I had a beautiful little girl that I loved very much. I was operating my own business out of my house, which allowed me to stay at home with my daughter at the time, and it was doing well. But one early morning, I got a call from a man who said he had heard about the products I was selling and wanted to come by to pick some up. I set the appointment, and he arrived shortly after nine, but it wasn't long before I began to feel uncomfortable about him being there. There was just something inside me that kept telling me he wasn't supposed to be there. So I quickly gave him what products he had purchased and got up to show him to the door. But that's when he grabbed me from behind and put a knife to my throat and raped me. Once again I found myself losing control of things, and I felt like that little girl again, helpless and horrified. But this time I found myself feeling more concern for my daughter than myself because she was only a few feet away from us asleep in her room. I knew I could handle whatever happened to me that day, but I don't think I could have handled something happening to her. But I did survive the attack, and God kept my daughter safe, and for that I will always be grateful.

But once again I found myself having to deal with more sexual abuse in my life and all the negative feelings and emotions that come along with it. It became harder and harder to suppress things down inside me. And as time passed, I found myself falling into a deeper depression. This was when I saw my biggest fear coming about. I began to see a change in my marriage, and the close relationship that my husband and I had once felt was now disappearing before my eyes, and I didn't know how to stop it. At the time I couldn't see that because of how I was feeling, I was the one causing all the problems in our marriage by the things I was doing and saying. I was always quick to put the blame on Freddy for everything, not realizing just how patient, supportive, and understanding he had been through it all. My focus had been all on me for some time, and because of this, I couldn't see that I had been putting up walls all around me, never allowing anyone, including Freddy, to get to close out of fear of getting hurt again or the fear of losing what we had in our relationship. And this left me feeling all alone and having to deal with all the burdens of life by myself. But I now see I wasn't dealing with things at all. I was just suppressing more junk down inside where there was no more room. And each day I continued to pretend everything was okay. But sexual, physical, and verbal abuse has a way of making you feel as if you have been stripped and robbed of everything that is important. And when this happens, you become desperate to hold on to the little you may have left of yourself. It was like I was fighting to hold on to my life, a reason for existing, and that is how I had been feeling for a very long time.

It was during this time that I found myself focusing more on my outer appearance. I needed something that I could see that would make me feel better about myself. And I guess you could say that in my mind I was thinking if I looked desirable I would be desirable and others would love me and want me around them. But no matter what I did or how much I tried, I was not able to find what it was that I needed. And normally I ended up feeling worse because of the disappointments I experienced. I now know I experienced those disappointments because I couldn't walk away from the battles that were going on in my mind. I had all these questions I had no answers to that my past had created. So instead of seeing things get better with time, I continued to see things get worse.

At the age of thirty-seven, I was diagnosed with breast cancer. During this time, they didn't have a lot of the drugs they have today. So when you were told you had cancer, you left the doctor's office feeling as though you had been sentenced to die. The cancer I had was a very aggressive and fast-growing cancer. So the doctor immediately recommended surgery and extensive chemo to follow. Over the next several months, the surgery and the loss of my hair because of the chemo left me with little hope of ever becoming a woman someone could love and desire. But I do remember praying and asking God to heal me of the cancer. I had seen firsthand just how difficult life could be, and I wanted so much to see my daughter grow up and be there for her if she had to go through difficult times. Just like my mother had been there for me. And God answered that prayer. But I still did not understand why he was allowing all this to happen.

As a little girl and then as an adult, I had heard many times that God loves us and can do anything. But my life experiences up to this point was telling me something else. Many times I had asked God these questions:

"If you truly love me, then why did you allow me to get hurt, which has caused me so much pain and sorrow that I feel today?"

"If you can do anything, then why didn't you stop my dad and others before they abused me?"

"Why did you allow me to come down with cancer?"

These are all legitimate questions and deserve answers. But it wasn't until God helped me by having me reflect back on my life was I able to begin getting some of those answers I needed, and see that he had always been there with me in the good times as well as the bad. Just like the time he intervened and my mother said she heard a voice telling her to go home, which put an end to my dad molesting me. When I was raped and became so afraid, I wouldn't leave my house, and God sent a friend that would pray for me and calmed my fears. And when God healed me of the cancer and allowed me to see my daughter grow up. He had always been there with me even though I couldn't see him most of the time. The memories of every time I experienced being hurt had become itched in my mind, and I didn't know how to erase them. And they become so much and so many that over time they were all I could see.

I believe that as we grow up and mature and become adults, we all have dreams and make plans and preparations on how we want our life to be. But because life is so unpredictable, and no one knows for sure what will happen from one moment to the next, life can sometimes leave us with a lot of questions that no one has an answer to but God. For most of my life, I lived with a lot of questions that I had no answers to, which caused a battle to go on within me that I could not win alone. In the mist of this battle, I grew tired and weary, and over time I began to lose all hope of ever being happy. By the time, I was forty four years old I felt like I couldn't fight no more. Neither did I want to. But it didn't seem to matter how I was feeling because life continued to go on. I had responsibilities that needed to be fulfilled each day as a mother, a wife, and now a child care business owner, and there seem to be no escape.

But in the year of 2001, I began to see things happen that would change my life forever. It was about four thirty in the morning on a midsummer day. I remember waking up that morning feeling angry and not really knowing why. I knew I had to go to work, but at the same time, it was the last thing I wanted to do. All the time I was getting ready, I could feel more anger building inside, and I didn't understand why. I just wanted to run away and hide somewhere and be by myself until it passed, because that was how I had dealt with things in the past whenever I would get to feeling like this. But I knew that wasn't possible on this particular morning. It was my responsibility to make sure the doors were open at 6:00 a.m. at the center. I loved working with the children, but this morning was different. I just felt trapped and felt like I was being forced to do what I did not want to do. You could say that the stress of everything—my past, my marriage, and my business—was all getting to be more than I could handle. I was also going through early menopause because of the cancer, and the two just don't seem to go together well.

I remember my sister, who was my director at the time, telling me just a few weeks earlier, "Barbara, the girls, meaning the ladies that I had working for me, are scared to be around you. They never know what kind of mood you are going to be in, so they just scatter when you walk into the room." I knew what she was saying was true, but I didn't understand why. I just thought they didn't like me and didn't want to be around me. It wasn't until she brought how I had been acting to my attention did I realize that I needed to do something or these ladies may end up quitting. After all no one likes working for the wicked witch, and you could say that was who I had become.

So out of desperation, I made an appointment to go and see a doctor. I explained how I was feeling and how it was causing so much tension at work. All the while, I was hoping she could give me some miracle drug that would make things better. Well, when I left her office, I left with a prescription for an antidepressant, which didn't seem to help much. So I went back to relying on my old tactics of suppressing and pretending. But by this time, there was no more room for junk.

Angry and sick to my stomach, I got dressed, threw everything in my car, and headed for work. It was about 5:30 a.m. by this time. When I was about halfway there, I remember just slumping down in my seat. I was feeling like I had been beaten up and defeated. And I began to cry uncontrollably, and that was when I cried out to the Lord in desperation. I remember saying to him that I was tried, and if this was the way my life was going to be, just take me out of the game, because I quit. In that moment, once again I felt like dying would be a lot easier than living because I felt like I had tried and failed at everything. And I felt like the burdens I had been carrying around for years had got too heavy for me to carry any longer. I knew in my heart that I needed God's help. And like a lot of people who become desperate, I made a vow to God by saying, "If you will make my life better, I promise I will begin each new day thanking you for the day you have given me. And I will look to you for advice on what I should do and where I should go." And I meant it with all my heart. I had spent forty years trying to change my life based on what I knew and had failed. I learned from my past failures and began to see that it had to be God who stepped in to change things in my life because not I or anyone else could.

It is hard to express with words how I felt when I finished that prayer. It was like everything in my life had been put on someone else's shoulders and the weight of the world had been lifted off of mine. I felt such a relief and a peace around and within me. And this caused the sadness I had been feeling just moments before to turn into feelings of joy, and I began to praise the Lord and have not stopped since. It was such a relief to have all the fears, worries, and concerns lifted off my shoulders, and in that moment, I knew in my heart that it was longer my responsibility to worry. I had turned everything over to Jesus.

I have since learned that God's greatest desire is to show us just how much he loves us and to have us love him back. But he will not force himself on anyone. We first have to ask; then he is faithful to do what he says he will do. Jesus tells us in Matthew 11:28–30, "Come to me, all you who are weary and burdened, and I will give you rest. Take my yoke upon you and learn from me, for I am gentle and humble in heart, and you will find rest for your souls. For my yoke is easy and my burdens are light."

John 10:10 says, "The thief comes to steal and to kill and destroy." And in the first part of my journey, he did a pretty good job of doing just that. But in the second part of that same verse, Jesus tells us, "I come so that they may have life and have it to the full." The God of mercy and the God of grace heard my cry that early summer morning. He came to my rescue, and now my journey continues full of hope for better days to come, hope that I can only find in Jesus.

As I close out this first chapter of my journey, I would like to summarize by saying that God created (Genesis 1:27) and placed us here in this world knowing all the good and bad things we would encounter (Psalms 139:16). But I have learned that he never intended for us to face them alone. I now know that because of God's love for me he allowed me to experience the things in my life, even though they were very difficult at times, so that we could be reunited together one day. And by allowing me to go through what I did he was able to help me take my first step out of the valley and begin to make my way to the mountain. He helped me to become humble before the Lord, acknowledging his glory, his majesty for he is the one who sustains all creation and realizing that I am nothing and can do nothing without him. Jesus tells us in John 15:5, "I am the vine; you are the branches. If a man remains in me and I in him, he will bear much fruit; apart from me you can do nothing."

Getting Acquainted with My Lord

I have said, as a little girl, Jesus became my Savior. But on that early summer morning, after years of trying and failing at having the life that I wanted, Jesus became my Lord and my Shepherd. In my prayer to him, I had made a commitment, a covenant with God. In exchange for a better life, I promised to acknowledge and spend time with him each day and let him make all the decisions concerning me. And now that our relationship had been restored, God used the next several months to allow me time to get to know who my new companion was, and begin to see and understand what a difference it would mean in my life to have Jesus as my Lord. This allowed me time to enjoy the peace he brings along with him as I regained my strength.

When we begin our journey together, I started each new day with him in prayer just as I had promised I would do. And that was the only thing I was doing differently in my life, but what a difference it made. My circumstances did not change immediately, but I began to see that my attitude was. My thoughts no longer consisted of what I could do, but what Jesus could do in me, through me, and for me. It was like I was experiencing a new birth with a second chance at life, just as it says in 1 Peter 1:3, "Praise be to the God and Father of our Lord Jesus Christ! In his great mercy he has given us new birth into a living hope through the resurrection of Jesus Christ from the dead."

As the days and weeks went by, the ladies at work began to question me on the changes they were seeing in me. This was a good thing because it allowed me to talk to them about God and what a difference he had made in my life. Before long, it seemed like that's all any of us wanted to talk about. The tension we had all felt previously was now gone. And for me, instead of dreading each new day, I was now beginning to look forward to the days to come. And I was giving God more praise than the day before because of what I was seeing him do. In a lot of ways, I felt like a newborn baby in the arms of the Lord. My every need was being taken care of, and it seemed as though every prayer was being answered. In the first part of my life's journey, I spent all my time putting up walls and not trusting anyone because of the fear of getting hurt. But God has a way of getting rid of those walls we create and helps us to get back what life in this world takes away from us. He did it for me by showing himself faithful, always being there for me when I needed him, and his actions

THE VISION

showed me just how much he loved me. Without trust I have found that it is really hard to have faith in anything or anyone, and I believe that God wanted me to have faith in him.

By May of 2002, God would move our relationship to the next level. He began to reveal to me things about himself that I had heard others talk about but had never experienced personally. This all began on a Thursday night while my husband was gone bowling. While I was sitting at home flipping channels on the TV, looking for something to watch, I ran across a program that got my attention. It was called the *Hour of Healing* hosted by Richard Roberts. Upon seeing this, I immediately began to remember a time when I was about seven years old and we were staying with my aunt in California. My cousin, who was a couple of years older than me, was watching Oral Roberts on TV one day, and when it come to the end of the program, he asked for anyone who needed healing to place their hands on the screen as he prayed, and she did. Afterward, I remember we asked her why she did that, and she said she believed God would get rid of a large mole she had on the back of her hand, and he did. That memory had gotten buried deep inside me. But I believe that God planted that seed in my life so on this night he could use it to get my attention long enough so he could reveal to me that he wanted and had the power and authority to heal me.

Out of curiosity, I continued to watch this program, and before long I heard Richard speak about someone at home that was having trouble with their hand,

35

specifically their thumb. I thought to myself, *That's me.* For some time, I had not been able to use my right thumb because of all the swelling and pain that had developed. Richard then said that he was going to pray and God was going to heal them. He then asked that whoever needed this prayer to place their hands on his hands, not because he had any power, but as a point of contact to believe God could and would heal them. I knew in my heart that I was supposed to do this, but at the same time, I didn't want anyone to see me doing it. So I jumped up and closed my blinds and shut my front door. As I went over and placed my hands on the screen and he began to pray, I felt warmth go through my hand, and I knew God had healed my thumb. I felt the pain leave immediately, but it took a couple of days before I saw the swelling go away completely. Before that night, I had experienced the love of God, but now he had revealed to me that he was a compassionate God as well, wanting to heal me of whatever caused me pain. He also allowed me to get my first good look at the pride that was living inside me. I did everything that I could so the world wouldn't see that I was trusting God to heal my hand, all because I feared how people would see me or what they would say about me if they knew.

In the NIV Bible, Matthew 9:35–36 confirms that Jesus is a loving and compassionate God when it tells us, "Jesus went through all the towns and villages, teaching in their synagogues, preaching the goods news of the kingdom and healing every disease and sickness. When he saw the crowds, he had compassion on them, because they were harassed and helpless, like sheep without a shepherd." Without me even realizing it at the time, Jesus my Lord had become my Shepherd, and he put an eagerness within me to learn all that I could about him. So I made a point to watch the *Hour of Healing* every chance I got.

By this time I was seeing my faith in God and my love toward him getting stronger. But I couldn't bring myself to tell anyone about how he had healed my hand. Again my pride and the fear of what others would say got in the way. I think it is safe to say that my way of thinking had been influenced by all the negative remarks I had heard about Oral Roberts and his ministry over the years. What I had heard caused me to feel like people wouldn't believe me, or think I was a nut like I had heard others say he was. But one night I heard Richard say that whenever God does something for us we should tell others. And when we don't we are denying God his glory. And in Matthew 10:32–33, it tells us, "Whoever acknowledges me before men, I will also acknowledge him before my Father, in Heaven. But whoever disowns me before men, I will disown him before my Father in Heaven." After all that God had done for me up to this point, denying him of his glory was the last thing I wanted to do. But I found out very quickly that laying down my pride wasn't that easy to do. And in most cases we cannot do it without God's help because of whatever fear we have inside us.

After much prayer and a few months, God did help me to lay down my pride and fears in this case. And I was able to share with a friend the miracle of healing he had performed on my hand. And together we praised God and gave him the glory he deserved. I have come to believe that I received the healing in my thumb because that was God's will for me, and I chose to believe that God could and would heal my hand. And it is still healed today. Matthew 8:13 tells us, "Jesus said to the Centurion Go! It will be done just as you believed it would. And his servant was healed at that very hour."

But God also showed me that what he had done for my cousin several years ago and what he had done for me had nothing to do with Richard or Oral Roberts, the men, but everything to do with him. It wasn't the men that made these things happen. They were just a conduit or a way so God could fulfill his plans in our lives. We see the same thing in the Scriptures when we read how God used Moses to deliver his people from bondage. And Joseph was used to provide for the people during a famine. And even Jesus, God's own son, was used so that we who choose to believe in him could be forgiven for our sins and be able to be reunited with God, and spend eternity with him.

I also learned during this time that there will be times of testing our faith. And God uses this time so we can see with our own eyes areas of our faith that need to grow, but also so we can see what he can do that we can't. In Matthew 8:13, it tells us, "If you believe you will receive whatever you ask for in prayer."

In September 2002, my faith was tested. God had healed my thumb on my right hand. But in just a few months, the same symptoms came back, only this time they were in my left thumb. The symptoms seemed to progress faster and were worse than before. And knowing what I had seen God do through the *Hour of Healing* just a few months earlier, I turned to the *Hour of Healing* again, expecting to see the same results, but nothing happened. For a new Christian who knew nothing, I was really confused at the time this was going on. I just remember saying, "Lord, I don't understand why you would heal my right thumb right away, and you did nothing about my left. But I have seen that you can heal, and I do believe that you will heal my hand." And I continued to pray asking for that healing. A few weeks later, as I was watching Richard, I heard him say, "Sometimes we may not see our healing right away, but we have to receive it by faith and do not doubt, and then we will see God's glory revealed." This statement encouraged me to continue believing in God for my healing even though more time had passed, and I had not yet seen any signs that healing would occur.

In October of 2002, about a month later, my mom, Freddy, and I were on our way to Kansas City for a weekend away. We were about halfway there, and I was staring out the window when I heard a low soft voice say, "Move your thumb." Again I knew in my heart that the time had come for God to heal my hand. With all the swelling, it wasn't much at first, but I moved my thumb the best I could. I was beginning to learn from watching the *Hour of Healing* and hearing God's Word that when we enter into a relationship with God, he is faithful to do his part, and he expects us to do ours. He will not do it for us. And when we do our part, that is when we see God's glory revealed. Our part is to have faith and believe in God. His Word tells us in Isaiah 53:5, "By His wounds we are healed." His Word did not say maybe we would be healed, but by using the word *are* I believe God is saying to all of us that a way for our healing has already been provided and all that is needed to bring it about is our faith. I have learned that to receive this promise or provision from God we do have to have the faith to believe it, and then back up our faith by acting accordingly. Without some kind of action to go along with our words, it leaves our words with little meaning. For example, we can tell someone all the time that we love them, but unless we are able to show them that love by the things we do, they will not believe what we say is true. In other words, it will be our actions that confirm the Word when we say "I believe." God told me to move my thumb, and this let me know he could and would heal it. But I believe that if I had allowed the pain I was feeling to stop me from doing what God said to do, I would have never seen my thumb healed.

By the time we arrived to where we were going, I was bending my thumb more and more. And by the time we made it back home, my thumb was healed completely, and I have never had any problems in my hands since. By this time, I was in awe of what God had done in me and for me. But it didn't stop there. I continued to see God heal whatever was wrong in my body.

There was one time when I was suffering from a really bad toothache and I would not go to the dentist because of fear. And yes the lack of money had something to do with it as well. After I had worked all day and dealt with my tooth hurting, by the time I got home, I was miserable. My husband had fixed a steak for us for dinner that night, and it really smelled good, but I couldn't eat. I don't know about anyone else, but when I experience pain for a while, I become desperate, and I will do just about anything to make it stop, especially when it is my teeth or ears that are hurting.

Well, after I had been at home for a while, I made up my mind that I was going in to take a bath and I wasn't coming out of the bathroom until God healed my toothache, and I didn't care how long it took. The medicine I had been taking wasn't working anymore, and I didn't have the money to go to the dentist. God had already showed me he could heal, and I wasn't taking no for an answer. As I went into the bathroom, my thought was, *How will I pray, I didn't have much experience on what to say to God like others who had been Christians for a while.* So I just started chanting what I knew to be true and that was, "Jesus can take away this pain." Over and over I chanted, and after a few minutes, I began to see this little red devil sitting on my shoulder, one like you would see in a cartoon. And as he sat there laughing I was hearing him say, "He's not going to do that." I knew God could because I had already experienced it. So I got angry and chanted even faster. You could say I was fighting the devil. I knew if I listen to him, he would cause me to doubt if God would heal my tooth. And doubt would rob me of God's blessing. The only way I knew how to drown him out was to chant faster and faster, which allowed me less time to think. I proceeded to get undressed and taking my bath, but I never missed a beat. As I am looking back on it now, it is really kind of comical. I had a pretty good rhythm going between the chanting and the lathering of soap. But as I began to rinse off the soap that I had lathered myself up with, I also began to feel the swelling going down. It was almost like it was being poured out of me. And as the swelling went down, I saw the pain begin to leave, and I felt the excitement bubbling up inside. My chanting then went from "Jesus can take away this pain" to "Jesus did take away this pain." And what made it even more exciting was I saw that with Jesus helping me I had fought the devil and won.

I was so excited and wanted to tell someone about what had just happened. But it was after ten o'clock at night, so I didn't feel I should call anyone. I had not yet started talking to Freddy about what God was doing in my life out of fear of how he would react. God and religion was not something that we had talked about much in the past. But the excitement I was feeling inside would not allow me to stay quiet. So I went to bed where Freddy was there watching TV. I didn't know how to start the conversation with him, so I just hulled off and hit him in the arm and said, "You might think I am crazy, but I have to tell someone what Jesus just did." Needless to say, it did get his attention.

I learned with this experience that God does not lie. Satan is the one who fills our heads with lies. And it is his lies that will cause us to doubt if God will really do what he says he will do for us. With this new understanding that God had placed in me I begin to see more clearly why faith is so important. Because it is the faith that we have in God and what he says he will do in his word that makes things happen in our life. And the more we see what God does in our life, the more confident we become in our future. And the more confident we are, the more determined we are to stand firm in our time of attacks and not give up. And we find ourselves with the ability to wait for the Lord to show up, and not miss out on any of God's blessings. I believe that God shows us an example of this type of confidence and determination he wants us to have through Jacob. For in Genesis 32:24–26, it tells us about how Jacob wrestled with God and would not let him go until he blessed him. He knew of God's blessings and knew God would bless him if he did not give up. And God did bless him because it goes on to tell us in Genesis 32:28 that God changed his name and gave him a new name, a name all people would recognize. For it says, "Your name will no longer be Jacob, but Israel, because you struggled with God and with men and have overcome."

There is one more experience where God healed me that I would like to share, and that is because of the lesson I learned. I had been having dizzy spells for a while. I never went to the doctor so I can't say what was causing them. But I can say they seemed to get worse as time went by. While I was at my dad's decorating his house for Christmas, I began to have some of these dizzy spells, and he began to fuss over me. He wanted to take me to the hospital and have it checked out, but I refused. During this time, he had not been the only one who had showed me their concern. And I am a little ashamed to say it, but I liked the attention so much, so I did nothing about the problem even though it meant I would have to suffer. But Jesus would not let me get away with this type of behavior.

Shortly after my dad left to run some errands, I began decorating the fireplace, and I started stumbling across the room. I couldn't seem to get my balance, and that is when I heard the Lord say, "You have not because you ask not." Immediately I realized he was right, and he let me know that what I was doing was wrong. When I finally made it over to the chair and sat down, I began to pray. I asked God to forgive me for acting so foolish, for looking for what I needed in others instead of him. And I asked for him to heal me of the dizziness. After sitting there for a moment or two, I got up and proceeded to decorate without any problems, and have never been bothered by the dizziness since.

God helped me to understand through this experience that when we lose that feeling of being loved it causes us to hunger for attention. So much so that we will normally do some pretty stupid stuff, even to the point of causing ourselves or others more pain and suffering. Therefore, a lot of the pain and suffering we experience is nobody's fault but our own. It is the things that we do or don't do trying to fulfill our selfish needs or desires that can sometimes make us feel as if we are in a valley. I now know that God wants to be our help, and I believe that if he cares enough to heal me of a toothache or a dizzy spell, he will want to heal me of anything that causes me to hurt. But I first had to have the faith to believe it. I believe that was what he was trying to show me during this time.

I now see that by God healing me of all the small things, he was able to begin the process of tearing down the walls I had created and restore my ability to trust again that my past experiences had taken away. But I have also seen that by God helping me to trust in him through his faithfulness to do what he says he helped me to take my second step that would lead me out of the valley. He developed my faith to believe in him and what he could do by all the things he was doing in my life. The Scriptures in Hebrew 11:1 tells us, "And faith is being sure of what we hope for and certain of what we do not see." And in Hebrew 11:6, "Without faith it is impossible to please God."

His Will

So far the year 2002 had been exciting. I was beginning to see and experience a god that was real to me. Always before, even though I believed in God, I never thought of him as being like me, someone who had feelings and emotions or who could experience joy, pain, or sorrow. He was just God. I think that is what happens with a lot of people. We know in our hearts that he exist, but because we cannot see or talk with him as we do others in our lives, it becomes really easy to ignore him, and we don't consider how he must be feeling.

But because of what God was doing in my life, it was really hard for me to ignore him. And by this time, he had won my heart and was consuming my every thought. It seemed like all I wanted to do was spend more time with him and sing praises to him. But I found this to be very difficult at first because growing up I never spoke much. I was always afraid I might say something that would reveal what was going on in my life, so I learned how to keep quiet. But keeping quiet doesn't allow us to learn how to talk, so whenever I would open my mouth to speak, all the wrong words seemed to come out. And this became very frustrating to me when I became an adult and found myself needing to speak, because I always ended up feeling like a fool, which did nothing for my self-esteem.

But when God clothed me with this new garment of praise toward him, the desire was so strong to talk to him and praise him. I began to buy every praise and worship tape I could get my hands on. I used someone else's words in the songs to say to God what I wanted to say and to express how I was feeling. I was beginning to see that I didn't deserve all that he was doing for me. And I found my heart overflowing with gratitude. Psalms 40:1–3 would become some of my favorite scriptures in the Bible because I could relate to the Psalmist when he wrote, "I waited patiently for the Lord; He turned to me and heard my cry. He lifted me out of the mud and the mire; He set my feet on a rock and gave me a firm place to stand. He put a new song in my mouth, a hymn of praise to our God."

Up until this time, God had been the one doing all the giving in our relationship. And I guess he knew that before things could go any further, I had to start doing something as well. It was toward the end of the year in the month of November that Freddy and I sold an old trailer we had on the lake. And one night after spending time with God in prayer, I heard the Lord say, "You need to start paying tithes." This really left

The Vision

me feeling confused because I had not attended church since I was a little girl, so I had no idea what tithing was all about. I had heard other people talk about it before but not enough to know what God was asking me to do. We were not attending church anywhere, so I had no one I could talk to about it, so I went back to the Lord in prayer looking for answers.

Before long, it seemed like every time I would turn the TV on to watch the *Hour of Healing*, Richard would be teaching on the importance of tithing. In a very short period of time, my questions had all been answered, but I found myself faced with another dilemma. While Richard was explaining tithing, I heard him say that we should always pay our tithes to the church we belong to. Well, at the time I didn't belong to a church, so I found myself going back to the Lord asking, "What should I do?" Again God was there willing and wanting to help, and he did lead me to pay my tithes to the Oral Roberts Ministries, because that was the church he had been using to minister to me.

My very first tithe was two hundred and fifty dollars, 10 percent off the sale of our trailer. But because we were struggling financially at the time, I will say it wasn't that easy to let go of the money. Even though I owned a child care center, I wasn't able to take out any money for our own personal use most of the time. It seemed like it took every dime just to pay wages and all the business expenses that occurred each month. But when I began this journey with the Lord, I had made up my mind to do whatever he asked of me, no matter how difficult it may be for me. I had spent my whole life doing things my way, and that had left me miserable. It was now time to do things God's way. My thought was, *I have nothing to lose, and everything to gain.*

When I begin to reflect back and seen that tithing was the first thing that God asked me to do, I was a little surprised. It seemed to me that he would have wanted me to get involved with a local church and then ask me to tithe. It was almost like he was trying to put the cart before the horse, and this got me asking why tithing is more important. In Malachi 3:10, it tells us, "'Bring the whole tithe into the storehouse, that there may be food in my house. Test me in this,' says the Lord almighty, and see if I will not throw open the floodgates of heaven and poor out so much blessings that you will not have room enough for it." God helped me see that because he loved me so much, he wanted to bless me in every area of my life. But before I could receive those blessings, I first had to learn how to give. And he used tithing as a way to get me into the habit of doing that. He also showed me that if we are able to obey him in paying tithes, giving up what is really important to us, our money, then he can see that we truly trust him to provide all our needs just as he says he will. Before Freddy and I started tithing, when Freddy's work was slow, we just couldn't seem to make ends meet. But since we started tithing, we have been able to do more with the 90 percent that is left over than we ever did when we kept the full 100 percent for ourselves. I have learned through this experience that by me paying my tithes each week, I am able to obey God by providing for his house, the church, and it can continue to grow.

And because of that, I am seeing him provide what it is I need for mine. When I begin to tithe, I saw God doing things that I had no knowledge of but would soon come to know as I began to read the Bible. And this is the second thing God would ask me to do.

Things were beginning to move at a little faster pace as far as what I was seeing God do. And toward the end of November, again after spending time with him in prayer, I heard the Lord say, "You need to start reading the Bible." The only Bible we had in the house was a large family Bible you would see displayed on someone's coffee table. And because I wanted to obey God, I tried reading from it at first, but I found it to be to awkward. So I decided to go to our local K-Mart store where I bought a small King James Version of the Bible thinking this would be a lot easier. But I found out very quickly that it wasn't so easy for me. With the way the wording was in it, I felt like I was trying to read something in a foreign language. And I wasn't able to understand at all what I had read. But I continued to try because that is what God wanted me to do.

After all that God had done for me, I wanted so much to please him. And he had put such a strong desire in me to learn all that I could about him; it seemed like every opportunity I had I was opening the Bible to read. But after a few weeks of reading and not being able to understand, I became frustrated, and I just closed the Bible and began to pray. I remember saying, "Lord, what good is it to read your Word if I can't understand what it is saying to me? Help me to understand." Matthew 5:6 tells us, "Blessed are those who hunger for righteous-ness for they will be filled."

I begin to see that when we pray according to God's will for us, his answers come very quickly. It wasn't much time after I finished that prayer, asking for understanding of the Bible, that whenever I turned the TV on, I would hear the scriptures I had just read being explained in a way that I could relate to and understand. Within about eight months, I had read the Bible from beginning to end, and I found myself understanding it more and more.

I can say that during that time, I felt God's presence stronger than ever, and the more I felt his presence, the more I wanted him near. By reading his words in the Bible, I saw changes taking place in me from within. And I began to see him through different eyes. Yes, before, God was a taskmaster, someone I called upon to fix all my problems when everything else failed. But after spending so much time with him in prayer and now reading his Word, getting to know him, I began to see myself falling in love with him. The Lord has led me to believe that God wants us to look at our relationship with him, not as what he can do for us, but with more intimate feelings, one like a love affair. For it tells us in Matthew 22:37, "We are to love the Lord your God with all your heart and with all your soul and with all your mind."

Before Jesus become my Lord and began to teach me how to love in this way by loving me, I was not able to obey God and his commands. Because I didn't know how to love in that way, I had spent forty years of my life being too afraid and being taught through my experiences that love hurts, it disappoints, and it is selfish and could not be trusted. But even though this was my way of thinking, for years I continued to have this battle going on inside me. My flesh was telling me to not allow love in my life because I would end up getting hurt. But my heart longed for the kind of love that would accept me for who I am, both good and bad. Through reading the Bible, I drew closer to God, and he fulfilled that longing, and I now know what it is like to be loved unconditionally. It fills you with so much joy and happiness that nothing else you will ever experience can come close to comparison. Jeremiah said it this way in 15:16, "When your words came, I ate them; they were my joy and my hearts delight, for I bare your name, O Lord God Almighty." I wish I could say what the exact day or hour or minute was when all this happened. But I can't. All I can say is it did happen.

I now see that before Jesus became my Lord, my life experiences had taught me to live a life of lies that was leading me further away from God. And the further I was away from him, the more miserable I became. I believe that God knew that before my life could change and I could begin to experience a life on the mountaintop, there were some things that needed to change in me. And he used his Word to undo what my past had done. For it tells us in 2 Timothy 3:16–17, "All scriptures are God-breathed and is useful for teaching, rebuking, correct-ing and training in righteousness, so that the man of God may be thoroughly equipped for every good work."

The Bible has become a part of my everyday life because I have seen that the more I read, the more I learn. The more I learn, the more questions I receive answers to and the more I understand the whys, hows, whats, and whens that life can throw at us. It lets me know what God expects from me and what I can expect from him and what I can expect from Satan, and this makes life so much easier. There are no surprises. But I think the most important thing the Bible has shown me is how God laid his life down for me and died so that I could live (Romans 5:8). Through his Word, he is teaching me how to lay my life down for him, dying to self and the things of this world so that I can spend eternity with him in heaven.

Even though a lot had already happened concerning God and what I was seeing him do. What would happen next would really take me by surprise. In the month of December, just a few weeks after God had told me I needed to read the Bible, Freddy and I arrived at the center about five thirty in the morning. We liked getting there early so I could make sure everything was ready before the children begin to arrive at six. And this day wasn't any different than any other day. We went in, turned on all the lights. I made a pot of coffee, I checked to make sure I had everything I would need for breakfast, Freddy went into the baby room where he watched TV, and I went to my office where I sat and read the Bible. Since I had started reading the Bible every day before work, it just seemed to make the days go a little smoother. But this morning, shortly after I had spent time reading, I heard the Lord say, "You and Freddy need to get out of debt." And my first thought was, *Do what, Lord? Where did this come from?*" What I had heard the Lord say had nothing to do with what I was thinking about or what I had just read out of the Bible, and I couldn't understand how this all came about. But before I could finish that thought, God showed me the vision.

What I saw was myself standing on a very long, narrow highway. And on each side of that highway, as far as my eyes could see, was nothing but flat, dry, barren land. And as I looked ahead, it looked like the highway would disappear into the sky. It was so long. But just before it would disappear, I saw a very sharp curve in the road. And that is when I heard the Lord say, "When you turn that curve, you will be debt free." I responded by saying, "Lord, how can that be? Do you know just how much Freddy and I owe in debts?" At that time, we owed right at eighty thousand if not more to different ones. But then I became very excited because Freddy and I had always struggled in our finances and now God had said that when we turned that curve we would be debt free. I guess I began to see dollar signs.

God has since showed me that when I first saw the vision, I saw it through the eyes of my flesh, meaning the ways of this world I live in. And this gave it a different meaning than what he intended for it to have. Even though I had learned a lot from him, there was more I needed to learn. And that leads to why he would ask me to do the fourth thing.

Because of what God was doing in my life, my excitement was beginning to spill over into the lives of the people around me. I could see God working in my sister Becky, her daughter-in-law Melinda, my mother, and my daughter Melissa. And by February of 2003, God would reveal to me the fourth thing that he would ask me to do. Again it was after spending time in prayer and reading the Bible that God said to me, "You need to start going to church."

Freddy and I had neighbors that had been attending church for a couple of years. And many times they had invited us to go with them, but for whatever reason, we never did. When God spoke to me and told me I needed to go to church, I knew our friends would be thrilled to have us go with them, but I just didn't feel that was where God wanted us to be.

My daughter was going through many difficulties in her marriage during this time, and during one of our conversations, the subject of God came up. I remember she started talking about a church that a friend of hers attended and said she was thinking about going. I told her I thought that would be a good idea, but I never once mentioned that God had wanted me to go as well. But I knew in my heart that it was only going to be a matter of time. Within a very short time, Melissa and my granddaughters did start attending Belview Baptist Church. And almost immediately, Melissa started asking me to go with her. I remember telling her in one of our conversations that when Easter came, I would go. Going to church wasn't part of my weekly activities, and even though I wanted to obey God, I found it pretty hard to change my routine. I had made a commitment to God to do whatever he asked of me, and now I had made a commitment to my daughter. I was spending a lot of time in prayer asking for God's help so I wouldn't

The Vision

let either of them down. In the meantime, I was talking to my mother, Becky, and Melinda about going with us when Easter Sunday came. But I would soon find out that God had different plans. About a week or so before Easter, Melissa and I were talking about how everyone was going to be going to church on Easter Sunday, and I heard the Lord say, "Why wait? Why don't you go this Sunday?" I couldn't come up with an excuse, so when Sunday came, I went.

    I hadn't come out and asked my husband to go with us yet. I guess I was afraid he would say no, and that wasn't the answer I wanted to hear. I had been praying a lot about it asking God to prepare his heart so when I did ask he would say yes. On the night before church, I called everyone to make sure that they were still planning on coming with us, and they all said that they would be there. I remember I woke up that next morning, and I was so excited because I was doing what God asked me to do. But I was also very nervous. I hadn't attended church since I was a little girl except for when I went for a funeral. And I knew that I couldn't put off any longer the question I needed to ask Freddy. As I went to get ready, I turned to him and said, "Are you going to go with me to church?" Almost before I could get it out of my mouth, he said NO! I just felt like crying. I wanted so much for us to start this new adventure together. I started to walk away, and I stopped and said, "I wish you would change your mind, I would really like to have you with me." As I went to take my bath, I started to pray again, asking God to change his mind. And when I returned to the living room where he was sitting, I could see by the look on his face that there was still hope. So I asked again, "Are you sure you want go with me?" This time his response wasn't no, but "I don't have enough time to get ready before you have to leave." I was so excited I responded by saying, "I will wait on you." Even if it meant we might be late, he was going, and that is all that matters. I felt like if I could get him to go this first time, he would continue to go with me in the future.

All together we had about nine people, all family sitting in church that Sunday morning. Some had been saved earlier in life but had drifted away from the Lord. For others it was their first time to attend. I felt in my heart that God led us to this church for a reason but at the time I didn't know why. But I would come to understand in the months and years to follow.

In this chapter of my journey, I will close by saying that during this time I saw even more of God's love and blessings being poured out upon me. And I began to see changes take place in me from within. He helped me to fall in love with him, and that changed the way I saw him and how I treated him. But he also helped me to take my third step that would lead me out of the valley. He helped me submit my life to the Lord and his will, by asking me to do what he wanted rather than doing what came natural to me.

Going Back to School

In a lot of ways, what we do with our children is what we can expect to see God do with us, because he is our Heavenly Father. For instance, we send our children off to school so that they can learn and grow in areas that will help them and make life easier when they become adults. I believe that God saw my reaction when he showed me the vision and knew I had a lot I still needed to learn before I could come out of the valley and have this life on the mountaintop and be able to share the vision with others in the way he wanted me to do it. So he enrolled me in his school by asking me to go to church, and he used the Bible I could study from as his textbook.

In early 2003, I began going to church just as God had asked me to. And all the people of Belview welcomed us as if we were a long-lost family member that had found our way back home. I guess you could say that's exactly what had happened, because for so many years we had been separated from God doing our own thing and living our lives according to the ways the world had taught us. But over the next seven years, God would use the people of Belview, the teaching of his Word, and the events in my life to open my eyes to see more clearly the person I had become, and the person he wanted me to be and grow and mature in my walk with him. He would also use the church as a place of refuge for me and my family, and it would be the place where he would bring healing hope and encouragement back into my life.

After attending church for a couple of months, Freddy and I were baptized together and joined the church. We both had been saved and baptized as children, and we knew that once you are saved, you are always saved. No one can take that away from you. But for me, I needed to be baptized again so I could confirm to God and to myself the commitment I had made two years earlier to make Jesus my Lord.

God did not waste any time because when I joined the church, he started to teach me the lessons I needed to learn. He had put a strong desire within me to sing his praises. But during this time that my daughter was struggling in her marriage, I found myself turning the music off whenever I would get into the car. I didn't understand why at the time, and it wasn't till after the fact did I realize God was preparing me so I could hear him when he spoke.

I remember I had worked all day from the time we opened until we closed that evening. It had been a very long and hectic day, so when everyone left, I quickly locked up and started for home. When I was about halfway there, I pulled up to a red light and just kind of sighed. After spending twelve hours around all the children—laughing, crying, and playing—it felt really nice just to sit there in silence. But that was when I heard God speak in an audible voice. It was almost like he was sitting in the seat next to me. And he said, "They're going to be okay, they're going to have they're trials and tribulations, but they're going to be okay. Now you need to go and apologize." Even though he didn't mention them by name, I knew who he was talking about and what it was he wanted me to apologize for.

Just a few weeks earlier, I took matters into my own hands and tried to fix my daughter's problems for her. She hadn't been out on her own for very long, so I felt like I still needed to take care of her. What I did was I confronted my son-in-law and let him know that we all knew he was cheating on Melissa. But I quickly saw that what I meant for good only made things worse, and for a long time afterward, I felt like Melissa resented her father and me for butting in. By me bringing it all out into the open, Melissa was forced to deal with the issue, and Scott, well, he just acted like he didn't have to hide things any longer, and this made things at home even worse for everyone. When God told me that I needed to apologize, because of how I felt about men in general because of my past, I responded to him by saying, "Lord, how can you ask me to apologize to Scott after all he has done to my daughter? And if I apologize, he will think that there is nothing wrong with what he has done." But immediately I heard the

Lord say, "It is not your place to judge him, that is my job. Now you need to go and apologize." It took me a while, but I did apologize for stepping in where I did not belong because I wanted to obey God. But I can say that it was not easy for me to do, and I couldn't have done it without God's help, because my thought was, Scott was the one who needed to apologize.

But to help me, God took away a lot of the negative feelings I had toward Scott by reminding me of some of the things I had done in my life that had hurt the people I was supposed to love. And even though what I had done and what Scott had done were nothing alike, he showed me that our actions caused the same result. People we loved still got hurt. By him allowing me to go through this experience, he helped me see that no one except God knows or understands why we do the things we do but everything happens for a reason, and that is the reason he is to judge others and not us. As I continued to reflect back on my life, I began to realize that the things I did that hurt someone else, I did not do intentionally. It was because I was hurting and searching for something I had lost. I had fallen into the trap of allowing my feelings and emotions to control my actions. I knew in my heart that hurting the people I loved was the last thing I wanted to do, but I did it anyway, not understanding why at the time. And this started me asking myself if the things that happened in my life caused me to do what I didn't want to do, was it possible that something had happened in Scott's life that no one else knew about, that was now causing him to do what he was doing? No one knows

THE VISION

but God, but the more I began to ask this question of others I encountered, the more I found myself not being so quick to judge. God helped me to understand this vicious cycle that we all seem to fall into through Paul's explanation of it in Romans 7:15–20, for he tells us, "I do not understand what I do. For what I want to do I do not do, but what I hate I do, I agree that the law is good. As it is, it is no longer I myself who do it, but it is sin living in me. I know that nothing good lives in me, that is my sinful nature. For I have the desire to do what is good, but I cannot carry it out. For what I do is not the good I want to do – this I keep on doing. Now If I do what I do not want to do, it is no longer I who do it, but it is sin living in me that does it."

Seeing my daughter get hurt was still hard for me, but I realized that God was in control of things, and I had peace because God had told me they were going to be okay. Through this experience, God helped me see the sin in my own life, and I learned a very important lesson. We are not to judge others because we have all sinned and fallen short of the glory of God, just as it says in Romans 3:23. And we are told in the scriptures by Jesus that when we are angry with someone, we are subject to judgment, the same judgment a murder would be subject to (Matthew 5:21–22). In other words, sin is sin in God's eyes and will be treated as such. That day I saw that because God loved me, he corrected me when he saw me doing something wrong that would hurt me and others later. And because he loved me, he gave me peace of mind concerning my daughter by telling me they would be okay. It was through my daughter's situation that God began the process of healing my inner wounds by emptying out the callous feelings I had in my heart toward men in general and began to replace it with compassion, the same compassion that he has for all of us. I never wanted to see Missy and Scott get a divorce and have my granddaughters grow up without their father being there. I just wanted Scott to love my daughter the way he promised and see them happy.

For a long time, I actually thought that Missy and Scott would be able to salvage their marriage. All because of what God had told me and because that is what I wanted. But they did end up getting a divorce, and they have all had to endure the consequences because of it. I think it has been harder on my granddaughters than anyone else. Children don't always understand what grown-ups do, so it is harder for them to accept. But as I am writing this book, Melissa has remarried, and the fellow she is married to now is making her very happy. And Freddy and I now have another beautiful granddaughter that we can love and spoil. Makayla and Marissa seem to be adjusting to their new family but still experience some difficulties concerning their dad not being there, all because in a lot of ways they are now experiencing what I did as a child, the lost time and love of their father. Only it came to them through a divorce instead of abuse. I know that it was because of God that they were able to get through this difficult time in their life, and will continue to get through what they may be faced with in their future. And I continue to pray for them each day, asking God to keep them close by his side, because I am seeing more and more what my mother said to me as a child is true. As long as we are in God's hands, we will be okay.

There were more lessons to be learned, so before long my mother, Melissa, Becky, Melinda, and I started attending a ladies' Bible study class that our pastor's wife Sue Branch had started in September of 2003. This allowed us to study God's Word in a more relaxed environment with mature Christian women. Even though I had learned a lot from the Lord since I began this journey with him, I was still an illiterate person when it came to God with a lot of questions that still needed to be answered.

When we first began, we had several ladies that attended our class, but over time, we began to see our attendance decrease in numbers. There was even times when I was fearful that Sue would discontinue them altogether. And this was something I did not want to see happen because I was seeing God work in my life concerning my past, and it was all good. Even though it was hard for me at times whenever he would bring up old memories that I had worked so hard to forget, I saw him answering many of my questions that I had been carrying around for years. And with every question that was answered, the more I understood why this all happened. With each new understanding, I found myself being able to let go more of my past. Earlier I had shared how God had healed my physical body. He was now taking care of and healing my spiritual one.

Even though our attendance dropped more and more over the years, Sue remained faithful to do what God had asked her to do, and our class continued.

And for that I am grateful today, because just as Sue continued to do what she was called to do, I saw God continuing to work in mine through the Bible study. And he healed my inner wounds caused from my past experiences. Little by little he took my life that had been torn apart because of the abuse and put it back together again. But the biggest and most important thing that I saw him do during this time was he taught me to love as though I had never been hurt by helping me to forgive those who had hurt me, and that is when I felt myself coming out of the valley even more.

As God continued to heal me, I began to realize that my focus was turning away from me and on to others who were hurting. And I found myself wanting to help them because I now understood what they were going through. From the very beginning, I had felt that the ladies' Bible study class was important, and by now I was seeing why. Because I had seen firsthand how God used the time we spent in his Word to bring healing, hope, and encouragement into the lives of the people he loved. And as I looked all around me, I could see that there was a lot of hurting people in this world, and everyone could use a little hope and encouragement especially in this day and time. And I knew from what he had showed me that we all needed his help.

Toward the end of the year, I began to see that God's purpose for the church wasn't just for a schoolhouse where his people would attend and he could teach them the things of him. But he also used it as a place of refuge where his people could receive comfort and support during difficult times, but he never stopped

THE VISION

teaching. By November of 2003, things became very busy around the child care center because we were preparing for the holidays. This year we were looking forward to Christmas because Jesus had become the main character in our lives. But without knowing it, all of our excitement and joy would soon turn into devastation and sorrow.

On the day before Thanksgiving, Becky and her husband Larry would open the center. Larry would sometimes come with Becky and would stay with her until it was time for him to go to work. But on this morning shortly after I arrived at nine, Becky received word that Larry had been in a car accident on his way to work and had been taken to the hospital. She immediately left to go and be with him. And since we had planned on closing early anyway because of the holiday, I began to call all the parents and ask them to come and pick up their children so that I could go and be with her. When I arrived at the hospital, I was told that Larry was in the intensive care unit and that he had an aneurism burst in his head while he was on his way to work. Upon seeing Becky and the grief and worry in her eyes, I knew things didn't look too good for him. I began to cry outwardly and inwardly for her and her children. Even though I had never experienced anything like this before, I believe a part of me knew how she was feeling, and I knew no words could take away her fear or her sorrow, so I cried and began to pray for all of them. I realized that day that God knew what Becky and her family was going to have to go through. Because he had allowed me to experience it for myself in a dream I had back in July with all the feelings and emotions she was now facing. I believe this happened so I would understand and be able to show her the compassion she would need in the days ahead.

In the dream that I had, I experienced my husband being badly hurt and was also admitted to the hospital and put in the intensive care unit because he had been shot. After he had spent a week there, he would die. But the dream did not stop there. It seemed like for weeks afterward I had to deal with the fear of being left all alone, not knowing how to live without him. And the feelings of loneliness and emptiness I felt were almost unbearable. The dream was so real that I woke myself up crying. And when I realized that it was just a dream, I was so relieved, but I spent the rest of the night with my arms around him crying and thanking God that it was just a dream. I learned from this that we may think we understand how others are feeling and be quick to offer our opinion on what they should do, but unless we have walked in their shoes and experienced what they have, none of us really know what they are in need of. I realized that even though God allowed me to have this dream and I experienced the fears and emotions in my dream that Becky was now facing, it could never be the same magnitude of fears and emotions she had to deal with at this time. Mine was a dream that I could wake up from and everything would go back to normal. But Becky's was real life, and nothing would seem normal for a very long time.

In the days to follow, Becky stayed by Larry's bedside hoping and praying for his recovery. During this time, she and her children had family, Bro. Tom, our pastor, and other people from the church praying for them and doing whatever we could to help. But after a few days, the doctors began to lose all hope that Larry would be able to pull out of it. And that is when they began to talk to Becky about taking Larry off life support. Becky was put in a situation where she had to make a very difficult decision. She knew that if she allowed them to unhook Larry from the machine, there was a possibility that he would die, and she would lose him forever, because the doctors had already explained all this to her. I just remember thinking, *How can anyone make that decision without God's strength and his help?* But on December 9, 2003, Becky did find the strength and help that she needed to make her decision, and she allowed the doctors to unhook Larry from life support. As we all stood around his bed continuing to pray, Larry would take his last breath shortly after he was unhooked from the machine. And all of us, who were left standing there in our sorrow and grief, could do nothing but sing "Amazing Grace."

I know that we all deal with grief in different ways, but for me, at this time, I found myself becoming very angry at God. I remember slipping away from everyone else and going to the chapel. As I sat there, I began to lash out at him by saying, "I don't understand why you allowed this to happen. I know that you can heal because you have healed me time and time again. But yet you did nothing to help Larry, why?" And that is when I heard God say in a very stern voice, "It is not your place to judge me or question my motives."

Immediately I felt like I needed to hide because I felt God's anger toward me, but there was no place I could go. I just remember falling to my knees, and I asked God to forgive me. God had already showed me that we are not to judge others. I learned on this day that we are not to judge God or question anything he chooses to do. That everything does happen for a reason, and in those times when we don't understand, God wants us to trust him no matter how hard it may be for us.

The next several months would be very hard for all of us, but it would be a life-changing experience for Becky and her children. All of them had to learn how to live without Larry being a part of their life. She needed time to grieve and time to figure out what she was going to do next. And this made things at the center a little difficult because that only left Melinda and me to run things. Melinda and I were struggling with grief as well because Larry was a part of our family. I guess it was at this time I started to see my business slipping away, because our mind was on everything but work. It was hard, but with the support and love of each other and God giving us the strength to endure, we did make it through this very difficult time. And we found ourselves now approaching a new year, and we were all thinking things could not be worse than what we had already experienced, but we were wrong.

By February 2004, just two months after Larry's passing, we found out that my mom had bladder cancer. I can remember the day we found out. My mom, my aunt Katharine, and I were sitting in Dr. Johnson's office waiting to hear the results of Mom's test. He came in, showed us the x-rays, and began to hem and haw around like he didn't want to say what needed to be said, and that was that they had found a tumor on her bladder. I remember looking at Mom's face and thinking, *He is not telling her something that she didn't already know.* I began to feel sick inside because I knew what she was about to face was not going to be easy. I couldn't help but remember how sick I felt when I had to take the chemo and how much weight I had lost during that time. And as I looked at Mom, I knew that she couldn't afford to lose any more weight because she only weighed about seventy-nine pounds. Even though I had said I never wanted to go through having cancer again, I wanted so much to be able to take her place. I knew she would need me to be strong so I could be there to help her. But I also knew that without God's help, that was not going to be possible. This was my mother, and the thought of losing her was scaring me to death.

We were all struggling with the fact that we had just lost one family member. And now we had to deal with the fact that there was a possibility we could lose another. Mom had started her chemo treatments, so I was spending most of my time with her. I guess God saw that someone needed to be at the center or the doors would have to be closed, and that would mean none of us would have a job. Becky had come back to work by this time, but she was still struggling with Larry's death, so she was just going through the motions. All of us were having such a hard time keeping our focus on work, and because of it, I saw our attendance at the center drop even more over the next couple of months.

By the end of May, Mom's health had really gotten bad. The side effects from the treatments were beginning to take its toll on her. And during my granddaughter's birthday party, we got a call from my dad telling us that Mom was nonresponsive. Immediately Becky and I rushed over to their house not knowing what we would find once we got there. Mom was still alive but would have to be admitted to the hospital. Just a few weeks before, I had made a promise to her to stay with her if for any reason she had to go into the hospital, so I had to follow through with my promise. I realized that by me spending all my time with her, I wasn't going to be there to take care of my business, but at the time, that didn't seem to be important. After Becky's experience with Larry being in the hospital, that was the last place she wanted to be, so she and Melinda agreed to run the center while I was taking care of Mom.

The next two weeks would be bittersweet for me. In the first week, I found myself glad to be able to spend all this time with her. All the time I was growing up, she cared and provided for me, and she was the one person in my life that loved me unconditionally. She never judged me but accepted me for who I was. And when I become an adult, my Mom become my closest friend. But by the second week, I began to see this woman who had always been so strong become so weak and helpless. And the woman who had always been there taking care of me, I found myself taking care of. Even though I could see her getting worse, I couldn't bring myself to give up hope. I think I prayed more during this time than I ever had before. My dad and I spent all our time by her side watching her have good days and bad ones. One minute we were experiencing hope, the next we had to deal with the fear that she wasn't going to make it. Our time at the hospital over these two weeks had left us exhausted, but we were still determined to be there to the end no matter what.

On Father's Day we were still at the hospital, and Dr. Baker, who was my cancer doctor, was making the rounds that morning. After examining Mom, she pulled me aside and told me it was time to tell Momma she could quit fighting, and that we would be okay. I explained to her that we couldn't do that just yet because we still had hope. But then she said to me that after her examination, she felt that the only reason why she was still with us was because she knew we were not ready to let her go and then proceeded to tell me I needed to let her go. Dr. Baker was a good doctor, and I trusted her completely, but what she had just said to me left me feeling as though what little hope and faith I had been holding on to had been ripped away. I was struggling with the fact that Mom had been after me for the last couple of days to take her home, but the hospital wouldn't allow me to do that. She had got so bad that they said she would never make it and they did not want to be held liable when she died on the way. Everything was coming to an end, and I didn't know how to make Momma understand why she couldn't go home, and I didn't want her to die mad at me. So it took me a while before I could discuss with my dad what Dr. Baker had told me we needed to do.

When I did get around to talking with him later that day, even though it was hard, we both decided that we did not want Mom to suffer any longer, especially because of our own selfish reasons. So I began calling all the family to the hospital, and once they got there, we had our talk with her. She seemed to be more alert and was doing a little better than earlier that morning. And with so many people there, my dad, Freddy, and I felt it would be okay if we stepped out for a short time and maybe got something to eat. None of us was really hungry, but because we needed some time to process what had been going on that day and what could happen, we went ahead and left. But as soon as we had sat down to eat, my phone rang. It was my daughter telling us that we needed to get back to Momma's room. I could tell that there was something seriously wrong by the tone of her voice, and we couldn't get back there fast enough. When I walked into the room, I knew we were too late. Mom had already passed away, and we were not there with her. I just remember sitting in the corner on a cot we had been sleeping on and feeling numb inside, in disbelief that she was now gone, and all I could do was cry. Bro. Tom, our pastor, was there going from one person to another trying to comfort us in our grief. And he was also helping us to make all the arrangement that needed to be made at that time.

I have said before that God led us to Belview Baptist Church for a reason. I just didn't know why. I was beginning to understand why. It took some time, but I realized even more just how much God loved us. We had no idea what was in store for us, but God knew, and he placed us in this church and among his people that would make our time of sorrow a lot easier to bear. And help us when we could not help ourselves.

Because of everything that had been going on, I soon found myself being pulled in all directions in the months ahead. Becky was grieving over the loss of Larry and Mom, and I was trying to help her. My dad was totally lost without Mom and was grieving, so me being the oldest of the children, I felt I needed to take care of him. But I was also trying to deal with my own grief, as well as take care of the business that was in danger of closing, and fulfill the responsibilities concerning my family. There was a lot of stress going on in my life, so when I did manage to get some free time, I spent it doing a lot of crying and praying. I had a lot of questions that needed to be answered, and I knew God was the only one that could answer them and give me some peace.

I felt such a void in my life when I lost my mother because we were so close, and I know that with time, that void gets easier to bear. But the concern I had about my mother dying angry with me would not allow me to move on. It seemed like the only time I was able to find any peace at all was during the time I spent with the Lord. But for the first few months after her death, all I could do when I was spending time with him was ask "Why did you heal me and not Mom or Larry?" I also needed to know that my mother wasn't mad at me any longer before I could find the peace that I needed to let her go.

One early morning, after spending time in prayer, I opened my Bible to read, and God answered one of my questions. I was reading in Isaiah 57:1 where it said, "The righteous perish, and no one ponders in his heart; devout men are taken away, and no one understands that the righteous are taken away to be spared from evil." Immediately after I had finished reading that scripture, I heard the Lord say, "They were taken away because I saw what Satan had in store for them. And I loved them too much to allow him to put them through that." When I heard this from the Lord, I felt as though I now understood the reason behind his actions, and it made it easier to accept. And even though I continued to miss them, I realized that because of the love I had for them, I too would rather let them go than to keep them here with me and see them suffer at the hand of Satan. I guess God wanted to confirm to me what he had said so there wouldn't be any doubt in my mind. When I arrived at our ladies' Bible study class that night, Sue our teacher told me that God showed her a scripture that she wanted to share with me, and it turned out to be the same scripture he had showed me earlier that day.

God had brought me peace concerning Mom's and Larry's death, but I was still struggling with the fact that I thought Mom was mad at me when she died and could not let that go. So I continued to go to him in prayer asking for that closure. And just as he was there before, he would also be there for me in this. He did that by allowing me to see Momma in a dream. When I saw her, she was sitting at the end of a long table with a smile on her face and her knees pulled up in her chair. That is the way she always sat at her table.

I could see other people sitting at the table with her but not well enough to make out their faces. And there was one standing at her side that I felt very strongly was the Lord. As I looked at her and then she looked at me all I could do was cry and say, "Oh Momma so much has happened since you have been gone." And I saw her reach out her arm as to welcome me and to comfort me, and I knew she wasn't mad at me anymore. But as I reached out to allow her to take me in her arms I woke up. But this time I woke up knowing that she was no longer mad, and I was able to find the closure that I needed and I just praised the Lord even more.

My love for Jesus grew stronger that day because of the love he had showed me. I had read in the scriptures in 1 John 4:8, "God is love" and in 1 Corinthians 13:8, "Love never fails." But it wasn't until I went through this difficult experience did I begin to understand what that really meant and the reason he commands us to love. I can now see that when our hearts our filled with love it destroys the selfishness and all other sin we have living inside of us that causes us to feel pain, sorrow and suffering, and wherever there are acts of love we find acceptance, peace of mind and are able to move on and we don't get stuck in the valleys.

It was during this experience that it became more evident that I served a God that was good and all that he did was good. But I lived in a world where Satan also dwells, and he is the spirit of evil always trying to steal our joy that we have found in Jesus. And because we live where evil lurks around every corner, we can expect to be affected by his evil schemes at one time or another in our lives. But in Romans 8:28, it tells us, "God works for the good of those who love him, who have been called according to his purpose." For me, when I read this and as I begin to put all the puzzle pieces together, meaning the things I was seeing God do in my own life, I realized that no matter what Satan may try to do to me, God would take what he meant for evil and turn it around for something good in my life. Therefore, I could expect to see something good in the end no matter how bad it may seem to be when it first began. And I believe that is why God tells us in Ecclesiastes 7:8, "The end of a matter is better than its beginning."

It seemed like the more we drew closer to God and began to do what he wanted, the more we were experiencing difficult times. I have come to believe that the reason was because Satan wanted us to question God and we would go back to our old way of living so in the end he could accomplish his goal of destroying us. But for Freddy and I, we held on to God believing he would see us through whatever would come our way. Becky wanted to believe, but she was struggling to hold on. Melinda did go back to her old ways. And before long she stopped going to church. She and Becky's son Carl got a divorce and had to give up their home. Because Becky was living with Carl and Melinda when they lost their home, she lost hers and had to come and live with Freddy and me. And none of us had a job any longer because I ended up closing the center on June 30 of 2005.

God has helped me see that the struggles my family experienced over the last year and a half is the reason most people have a hard time believing in him. We get caught up in our hardships and forget or begin to doubt what he can do or will do. But he has helped me to understand that he uses our struggles to get us to stop looking down away from him, and start looking up at him. In the past, I looked at my troubles as stumbling blocks, things that were preventing me from having the life that I wanted. But he showed me that they were actually stepping stones to get me where he wanted me to be, and that is on the mountaintop.

The rest of the year seemed to calm down somewhat. Since Becky was living with us and neither one of us was working, we had a lot of time just to sit and talk. And most of our conversations consisted of what we had been through and what we had seen God do during that time. I believe it was a time for healing for both of us. We all continued to go to church, and I believe that if God had not been able to minister to Becky through the church and his Word, she would not be in the relationship with him that she is today. This time was very enjoyable for me because I was able to spend more time with my granddaughters, who were six years old. And I was able to spend more time with God. I had already read the Bible a few times, but now God had put a desire within me to know the Bible, so I began to memorize some of the scriptures. By memorizing the scriptures, I saw I could have God's Word with me no matter where I was or what I may be facing. And Psalms became my favorite book in the Bible because just like the songs, I found it really easy to use the words of the Psalmist to talk to God and let him know how I was feeling. Before I knew it, I had memorized Psalms 1, 23, 40, 91, and103, and later I would add Romans 8 and Ephesians 6 to the list. I don't know why I choose these particular scriptures to memorize, but I can say they played a very important role in my life in the things to come.

The Vision Returns

Because of how my past had took over control of my feelings and emotion, it had caused me to become a very independent person over the years out of fear of becoming vulnerable and getting hurt. But because of that independence, I reflected a person that was strong and capable of making all the decisions. And that is how the people in my life treated me, even Freddy to certain extent. But when we become the decision maker, we begin to carry on our shoulders a lot of burdens, worries, and responsibilities that if we're not careful can make us feel as if we are carrying around the weight of the world. I believe that was one of things that I was having problems with when I cried out to the Lord for help. On that early summer morning, I had got to a point in my life that I wasn't able to take care of myself, so I couldn't make the decisions or take care of anyone else. I was in need of someone to make all the decision and take care of me, and the Lord was the one who agreed to do that.

But because the Lord had been doing this for a while, and I was enjoying the peace of mind of not having to worry about those burdens, I guess it would be safe to say that I got comfortable and began to take advantage of the situation. Because when I closed the center, I made up my mind that I wasn't going to be the one that worried about our bills any longer and try to figure out how they were going to get paid. I would turn those burdens over to Freddy and let him take care of it. To justify my decision, I told myself that he was the only one working now, so he should have the say on how the money was to be spent. Looking back, I can see how this was a very selfish move on my part. I knew how I felt when I was put in that position, but because I didn't want anything to rob me of the peace I had found, I turned the burdens over to Freddy anyway. I now see the mistake I made. I was trusting in Freddy to take care of our finances and bills instead of relying on the Lord.

The beginning of 2006 would be no different than any year since Freddy and I got married. We were in the middle of winter, and wintertime meant that Freddy didn't have much work, and that meant we would have to struggle in paying our bills. I can say that since we started paying our tithes, we still struggled at times, but they weren't as bad as before, because God always seems to provide what we needed when we needed it. By God allowing Freddy and me to experience what would happen in the days ahead, he continued to show me that there were things in me that still needed to change and taught me new lessons, and reminded me of old ones and helped me to begin understanding the vision and its true meaning. Because of what was going on inside me, over the years it had caused Freddy and me to become distant, and our relationship suffered from lack of communication. But during this time, God was able to help me see that when he brings a man and woman together in marriage, they become one. And when one tries to do something without the other being involved, it normally ends up creating more problems for them.

Well, by April of 2006, I began to see the problems my decision to allow Freddy to take care of our finances alone had created. I received a call from our bank, and the man on the phone said, "Barbara, did you know that you have a judgment against you? And because you have this judgment, we are going to have to turn over all the money you have in your account in just a few days." I didn't understand what he was talking about. Freddy had not mentioned any problems or showed any concerns about our finances, so I assumed everything was okay. I knew we had money in the bank all this time, so I didn't understand what the problem was. It wasn't until we started talking did I find out that he had taken out a loan and was not able to pay on it when his work slowed down. And I saw that because the money we had in the bank was in an account that I had opened, and we were not talking to one another concerning our affairs, he didn't feel he could take out any money for bills even though his name was on the account.

We then had a man show up at our house just a couple days later, and he proceeded to tell me that we were three months behind on our house payments and was in danger of foreclosure. It seemed as though we were being hit from all directions. In just a short period of time, everything went from being okay, so I thought, to Freddy being out of work, we had no money, and we were about to lose our home. I found myself becoming very angry and looking for someone to blame. And that someone just happened to be Freddy. I had heard my pastor talk on the subject of marriage and heard him say that God created the man to be the head of the house and leader of the family. But during our time of struggles, I couldn't see that Freddy was fulfilling that role. We had got to a place in our life that we had stopped talking and sharing with one another the things we were doing or what we were thinking. So because of that lack of communication, I just assumed he was doing nothing about our problems. I think that God used this experience as another way of helping me see that when we don't understand something, we can, and most likely will, make the wrong assumption about it. But through God's teaching and correcting, he helped me see very quickly that he wasn't too happy with my attitude or my actions toward Freddy. And with time and by using his words in the Bible, he showed me that what I failed to see is that yes he created the man to be the head and leader of our house, but he created me, the woman, the wife, to be his helper (Genesis 2:18). And I wasn't being of much help to Freddy with my attitude or my way of thinking. Once again he had to show me that I had gone back to my old habits of blaming others when things didn't go the way I wanted them to, never stopping to think that maybe I had something to do with the problem as well. God reminded me that because of the decision I had made to not have a part in this relationship and do what I could to help out with our finances, even if that meant just to support and understand Freddy's struggles, then we were going to have problems, and neither one of us was going to be happy.

I began to realize that because of our lack of communication with one another, we had both made some bad choices along the way. And because of those bad choices, we were now suffering the consequences. Once we started talking and working together again, we did manage to get things taken care of with God's help, but that peace didn't seem to last for very long.

We had now found ourselves in the middle of summer, and the summer normally meant we were doing well in our finances because Freddy's work was pretty steady. But this year we were confronted with something we were not expecting. Just a couple of years earlier, Freddy and I were trying to do what the Lord said we needed to do, and that was get out of debt. So we decided to refinance our home and set it up on a fifteen-year note instead of a thirty-year so we could pay it off sooner. But what the bank failed to tell us or make clear to us is that after five years, the loan would mature and if for any reason our credit wasn't any good, we would have to pay a very large balloon payment or lose our house. Well, this was the year the loan matured, and with everything that had just happened our credit was now no good. And in July we did receive the letter telling us we would owe that large balloon payment come November.

The vision had given me new hope and something to focus on as God was doing the work in me and my life. And I had been holding on to it with all I had inside me through all the difficulties we had faced so far. I believe that is what helped me to get through those rough times. But when we are struggling with our finances, it just does something to us that will make us think and act in ways that God did not intend for us to. I have heard it said that the lack of money is the cause for most divorces, suicides, and crimes in our country. And I believe the reason is because we know that without money we could not survive, because everything we do, own, or have to have to live we have to have money for, and when it is not there, we begin to experience fear of not knowing how we will make it.

When we received the letter telling us that we would owe this large balloon payment come November, once again I took my eyes off the vision and off Jesus and what he could do. And I began to experience this fear of not knowing how we were going to survive. Even though I was trying to keep a good attitude, I knew in my heart that there was no way we could come up with that kind of money in such a short period of time. And fear won me over, and I soon saw my attitude and actions saying, "Why even bother to try, it won't do any good." In other words, I was giving up again. It seemed like since the first of the year, all we had done was worry and try to come out of the financial mess we had found ourselves in. And I was so angry and just wanted to find that peace I had experienced just a few months before.

But God continued to be with me even though my attitude stunk, and he knew what I needed to get me out of this place I had found myself in, and he showed me the vision again. The first time I saw the vision, it gave me a promise, for it said, "When you turn that curve, you will be debt free." But this time it gave me hope and encouragement because what I saw was the same highway as before, but instead of seeing myself standing a long way off from the curve, I was now standing right at the curve, like I was getting ready to turn. And that is when I heard the Lord say in a voice that sounded like he was pleading with me, "Don't give up, see you are about to turn that curve." By him showing me the vision again, he refocused my eyes back on him and helped me to realize that things are not always as they seem. I saw that even though my circumstances were telling me I was not making any progress, the vision showed that I was moving forward and getting closer to turning the curve just as he said I would. I began to feel the hope rising up again inside me, and with the hope now restored, I found the will and courage to go and talk to the bank about refinancing our home. I just remember praying and asking God to go before me and prepare the way so when I did talk to the people at the bank we would get the answer we needed to hear.

Even though in my mind I was still thinking that they wouldn't renew our loan because of our credit, in my heart I was once again trusting God to make everything turn out for my good, and I was following it up by what I was doing. By this time, after all I had seen God do, I should not have been so surprised when the bank did agree to refinance our loan, but I was. But once again, I saw with my own eyes what God could do, and it made me even stronger in my faith. God helped me see through his scriptures and this experience, that money can be the root of our destruction if we are not careful. And if we are not careful, because money is so important to us, it can become our god, controlling how we think and the things we do. And he tells us in Matthew 6:24, "No one can serve two masters, either he will hate the one and love the other, or he will be devoted to the one and despise the other." And then he goes on to tell us, "You cannot serve both God and money." He wanted me to see that even though I thought I had given Jesus Lordship over my life, I was still allowing money to be my god in many ways. And money represents the things of this world and the one who lives in it, which is Satan. And he allowed me to see how he was using money to destroy mine and Freddy's happiness. But through what I just saw God do with the bank he reminded me that when I put my trust in him to provide he is faithful to do what he says he will do. He reminded me through his words found in Philippians 4:19, and through his works, that my God will meet all of my needs according to his glorious riches in Christ Jesus.

In the midst of God teaching and correcting me, he also continued to bless me. On top of everything else that had gone on so far this year, I was turning fifty in October. I know for some people, turning fifty is not such a big deal. But for some reason, it was really bothering me. I have always felt it was important to acknowledge someone's birthday, because by doing so you can say a lot to them that we may not say otherwise or acknowledge their value. For instance, it is a way for us to tell them that we are happy that they were born, and we are glad to have them as part of our life. I guess the reason I was having such a difficult time was because a week before my birthday, I wasn't feeling very valued by my family. I was feeling as though they didn't really care if I was there or not. And when we begin to feel as though no one cares, it can throw us into a "poor, pitiful me" type of attitude, and that is what robs us of our joy and happiness. I found myself thinking about my mother a lot at this time. I guess because I knew that when everyone else got caught up in what was going on in their life, she was the one person I could go to that could make me feel as if someone cared. I knew I couldn't have her with me on my birthday, but I couldn't stop thinking how nice it would be to receive a present from her as I had done in the past. And that was when I began to have the desire within me again to have Momma's rings.

When Mom passed away, I wanted to have her rings as a keepsake, and it would be something I could pass down to my daughter and granddaughters that was hers. But my dad was having such a hard time when we lost Mom, and he was finding comfort by sleeping with her rings under his pillow, I couldn't bring myself to tell him that I wanted them. No one else knew what my desire was, but God knew. Psalms 37:4 tells us, "Delight yourself in the Lord and he will give you the desires of your heart." I saw God fulfill another one of his promises in my life because on the day before my birthday my dad told me that he thought it was time for me to have Momma's rings and gave them to me. I knew without a doubt that this had all happened because God made it happen. My dad didn't do this because it was my birthday. He had forgotten all about it. But God showed me that he hadn't forgotten, and this made it a birthday I will always remember and cherish in my heart. Because at the time when I was feeling like everyone else didn't care, God allowed me to receive a birthday present from my mother who had been gone for a while.

God helped me see that life is good but it can be very difficult at times. But when we make him part of our lives and because of the love he has for all of us and He care for our well-being, we can expect to see his grace and know that his grace are blessings even when we don't deserve it. And those blessing will outweigh the bad things we encounter, filling us with peace and joy that surpasses all understanding. First John 1:16 tells us, "From the fullness of His grace we have all received one blessing after another." And in Philippians 4:7, "And the peace of God, which transcends all understanding, will guard your hearts and your minds in Christ Jesus."

The blessings I was seeing take place in my life was like a recess time from the classroom, but even in the time of blessings, I continued to learn. Over the next couple of years, I continued to learn and receive more wisdom and knowledge that would help me share the vision when the time was right. But in the meantime, Becky remarried in May of this year and had moved about an hour and a half away. So we didn't see each other as much, but we continued to talk to one another on the phone several times a week. I went to work for a temp service that had me working at a couple of different places. But it was mainly a time where God continued to heal me of my past and teach me what I needed to learn. I was spending a lot of time reading the Bible, which meant I was spending a lot of time with God.

A Time to Celebrate

I had always hoped that I would have children one day. But when I become pregnant with my daughter, that is when I experienced a joy like no other I had ever experienced before. But it wasn't until I knew for sure that I was pregnant did I begin to expect to see the birth of my daughter. And when I began to expect, that was when I began to experience the joy the anticipation of her birth brought into my life. The nine months that I had to wait for her to grow and develop was not always easy for me, because there were changes going on in my body. But those changes and the time I had to wait didn't rob me of the joy I was feeling because I knew eventually I would hold her in my arms, so I was able to endure. In the first few months of my pregnancy, there was no evidence that anyone could see that my daughter even existed. But even so, the things I was doing and what I was saying said that she did.

I share this as an example to show what God was doing in me over the past eight years through all the encounters and experiences. He was developing my faith to where I was now sure of what I had been reading in the Bible so I could expect to see it come about in my life just as he said it would. But there were some changes that needed to take place in me first. Healing needed to happen before I could come out of that valley. By this time in my journey, God had moved me to a place he wanted me to be. I was now expecting. I began 2009 with this new feeling of expecting to see something good happen in my life. And each day I found myself being filled with the same joy I felt when I was waiting for my daughter to be born. I didn't know what I was supposed to expect exactly, nor did I know when it would come. I just knew in my heart that something good was going to happen, so I got up each day looking for it wherever I went and in everything that I did with that same anticipation I had when I was pregnant with my daughter.

I also found myself not focusing so much on the negative around me anymore, but I was beginning to search, trying to see something good in all people I encountered and in circumstances that seemed to be difficult. I had seen firsthand that every time God did something in my life, it was good, and I remembered how happy it made me feel. Happiness was what I was longing for, so it only made sense to me that if I could see something good in the midst of the bad, the bad things could not rob me of my joy. The feeling was so strong inside me that I could not help but talk about it to others. I just remember going round saying, "Something good is going to happen this year, I don't know what or when, but something is going to happen." Even during the winter months when Freddy and I were struggling with paying our bills, I felt an inner peace and joy that could not be explained.

It was toward the end of July, and I had just finished spending time reading the Bible and in prayer. And as I was sitting there on my couch in silence, I heard the Lord say, "Draw the vision on paper." The first thought that came to my mind was, *Becky is the artist in our family, not me.* But I got a piece of paper and a pencil, and I began to draw what I had seen the best I could. The moment I finished the drawing, I saw with my eyes and then heard, "It is the Lord's staff." Immediately I could see all the scriptures that I had read in the Bible swirling around in my head, sort of like the clouds do when a tornado begins to form. And then they all come together in one place and landed on Psalms 23, (1) "The Lord is my Shepherd, I shall not be in want. (2) He makes me lie down in green pastures, He leads me beside quiet waters, (3) He restores my soul. He guides me in paths of righteousness for his name sake. (4) Even though I walk through the valley of the shadow of death, I will fear no evil, for you are with me; your rod and your staff, they comfort me. (5) You prepare a table before me in the presents of my enemies. You anoint my head with oil; my cup overflows. (6) Surely goodness and love will follow me all the days of my life, and I will dwell in the house of the Lord forever." I had experienced the joy of the Lord in the last several years, but the joy that I felt that day in that moment was beyond anything I could imagine. I felt like God had turned the key in the door of the prison I had created in my mind, and I was now completely free from my past. And I knew in my heart that it could not torment me any longer in my future.

In that moment, I went from seeing the vision through the eyes of my flesh, the way the world would see it, to seeing it through the eyes of my spirit, the way God sees it and wanted me to see it. And it took on a whole new meaning. I saw the highway that I was standing on turn into the Lord's staff right in front of my eyes. And this allowed me to see that through Jesus all things are possible. And I saw with my own eyes that God had sent Jesus to be my Shepherd, and I realized that just as he held the staff in his hands, I had been in his hands as well because I was on that highway. Many times I had read that God holds us in his hands. But it wasn't until God allowed me to see it with my eyes did it become real to me, and then I was able to experience what it feels like to be a child in the Lord's arms. God spoke to my whole being on that day and let me know that he had been with me all along and that my search was now over and that I had finally found what I had been searching for, for so many years. And that was the love of a perfect Father and all it represents (Matthew 5:48). And he has led me to believe that the reason he connected the vision to Psalms 23 is because the vision is for everyone just like the Bible and Psalms 23 is a mini-Bible in itself. It is about the Messiah that was to come in the Old Testament and the Lord and

Shepherd in the New Testament that is one and the same, Jesus. He allowed me to see that through Jesus he could demonstrate the fullness of his love for me (John 17:26). And through the works that I would see Jesus do in my life, I would understand that he is for me and not against me, so I did not have to fear (Romans 8:31), and that he desired to show me just how much he loved me by doing more for me than my earthly father ever could. Through Jesus, God is able to fulfill every promise that we find in the Bible no matter who we are or what our circumstances might be. I now know in my heart that whoever believes in the Christ our Lord and our Shepherd will find their way out of the valley. And while on that highway, we are in the arms of the Lord who came to us to do the will of the Father, and he promises to protect, provide, and bless us with every good and perfect gift (James 1:17).

Yes this was a time to celebrate because I knew I had come out of the valley I had been in for over forty years, and I was free to live on the mountaintop where God was leading me, safe and secure in Jesus's arms until the day that Jesus could place me in the arms of my Heavenly Father.

Upon seeing the vision this third time and feeling as though I understood its true meaning, I felt that the time had come for me to do what God had wanted me to do, and that was write about it in a book. But again God had other plans, and this would mean that there were more classes to attend and more lessons to learn. During this time, I found myself praying asking God to show me how I might begin to help others and share what he had showed me concerning the vision. And once when I was praying a similar prayer, almost immediately my niece Kristie came to mind. I remember saying, "Lord, how can I help Kristie? I don't even know where she is at."

Well, by the end of August, while I was sitting in my living room talking with our neighbor and friend Linda, a car pulled up, and Kristie got out. I was a little surprised to see her show up at my house. I hadn't seen or talked to her in months. I knew she must have been in trouble because she never came to my house just to visit. I also remembered the conversation the Lord and I had previously, especially the part where I told him I didn't know where Kristie was. I couldn't go to her so he brought her to me. I know I had asked the Lord to allow me to help others who were hurting. But when the opportunity came, I struggled with it big-time for a number of reasons. I knew from past experiences with Kristie that she wanted one or two things, money or a place to stay. In that moment, I had to choose what my response was going to be. The questions I was faced with was, "Am I going to do what I knew God wanted me to do, which meant I was going to have to give up something. Or was I going to turn her away so that I didn't have to endure the sacrifice." In the time it would take for her to get to my door, I had a lot to ponder over in my mind. If she asked for money, I could give it to her, but that would mean Freddy and I would have to struggle. Because what little we had we were using to live on. If she asked to stay with us and I said yes, I knew she could be there for a while, and I wasn't sure how Freddy would react to that. And I knew that once I said she could stay, I would not be able to ask her to leave unless she had a place to go. My flesh was telling me to say no to her request, but my heart was telling me to do what God wanted and that I would not be sorry.

I had learned from reading the Bible that God's principles for life was based on the example of seed time and harvest. And this meant that whatever seeds we plant, seeds like love, money, or time, etc., we could expect to see those things return to us whenever we're in need as our harvest, a blessing from him. But he has showed me that with every blessing, someone has to pay a price.

When I saw Kristie's face, I knew what my answer was going to be. I saw a young lady scared, hurting, and reaching out for help, and there was no way I could say no to her no matter what she asked. I knew in my heart that since God brought her to me she was supposed to be there, but the question I had to ask myself, was I going to trust him to provide for both of us what it was we would need? We spent the rest of the afternoon talking, and as I listened, I heard her say that while on her way to a women's shelter, she heard, "Go to your aunt Barbara's." When I heard this I knew for sure that it was God's will for her to be here. And I ended up telling her she could stay, praying that Freddy would understand. And it wouldn't cause any problems between us.

Originally it was just supposed to be Kristie that would be staying with us. But a week after she would move in, her three small children would also come to stay. Over the next four months, we all experienced some things that we were not used to and had to make some adjustments in our lives. But with God's help, we were able to manage, and Kristie was able to get the help she needed at the time. She was able to get a job, and that enabled her to pay off some of her fines. She was able to get her driver's license reinstated. She would also attend church while she was living with us. And before leaving our home and returning to live with her husband Kenny, he was saved and baptized. God also helped Freddy and me to grow in areas that we were the weakest, and that was being patient and walking in love and understanding toward others.

For Freddy and I, we had to sacrifice our time, money, and home. But the things we gained from that sacrifice blessed us in more ways than one. We were able to be a part of what God was doing in Kristie's life and experience the joy that comes from being a blessing to others. But God also blessed us by sending a buyer for the center. And with the money we received from the sale, we were able to pay off six of our creditors, which got us closer to turning the curve financially.

I believe I grew and matured a little more in my walk with God because I saw a little more clearly why he asked us to love others as we love ourselves. The way we treat others can be the determining factor on whether or not they come out of the valley or fall deeper into one, and it will determine what will happen in our life as well. During the time that Kristie and her children were living with us, God kept leading me back to 1 Corinthians 13:4–7 where it talks about love and the definition of love. The more I read God's definition of love, the more I realized there were some things I needed to work on before I could obey him and do what he commands us to do. Every day I see myself facing a battle with my fleshly desires and my old habits, and they didn't always include being patient or kind. There was more, but I won't mention all of them. I knew that all these things would not be easy for me to change because all my life I had been taught that if everybody is doing it, then it's okay. But I wanted to obey God, so I saw that I had to choose to do what didn't come natural for me and then look to God for help when I couldn't do it on my own. In Mark 14:38, it tells us, "Watch and pray so that you will not fall into temptation. The Spirit is willing but the body is weak." Every day I see myself facing battles with my fleshly desires and old habits. But more and more I am choosing what God desires and looking to him for help. I am seeing that even though it might sometimes be difficult for me alone to be patient, kind, and considerate toward others, walking in love as God commands us to do, with God's help it is possible, and I come away feeling less guilt because of something I have said or did. I like how that feels, so I find myself choosing to do it more and more.

Turning the Curve

The year 2009 had ended with high expectations. We had sold the commercial property we owned, which allowed us to pay off a very large portion of our debt. And for the first time in a long time, I didn't have to worry about having money for Christmas. But after the first of the year, it seemed as if someone had pushed the Replay button in our life. And we found ourselves going around that same old mountain I will call financial despair. After paying off our creditors, there wasn't much money left over, and it was winter, and Freddy wasn't working again. But I have to thank God for what little money we did have, because that is what helped us to get through.

We don't always like the way God provides for us. I was really hoping that we would be able to hold on to what little money we had so Freddy and I could take our granddaughters to Sea World come June. We had always wanted to do that but never had the money when it came time. And because we had to spend all the money on bills, I will have to say I was feeling a little down and disappointed because of it. I once heard someone say, and I wrote it in my Bible, "Unhappiness doesn't come because of the way things are; rather unhappiness comes because things are not the way we think they should be." I guess God saw that I would be needed elsewhere, and this was not the year for a vacation, and he would do what was best for all concerned. But even though I began the year feeling a little disappointed, it wouldn't last long because God would continue to bless me and let me know he was still there with me.

One night toward the end of January, I remember going to bed, and for some reason I began to remember the day Jesus became my Lord. I was remembering how I felt before he came to my rescue and how I felt afterward. And I began to think that it would really be nice if I could write a poem as a way to show the Lord just how grateful I was for all he had done. Sort of like the Psalmist did in the Bible. But as I said before, I wasn't very good with words and didn't have a very creative mind when it came to doing something like this. Becky was the one in our family that seemed to have this kind of talent. But the desire was so strong I think I was awake most of the night trying to come up with something. I woke up the next morning expecting to be really tired, but I found myself feeling pretty good.

After I had spent some time reading my Bible, the urge to work on the poem came back. So I began to put down on paper what I had come up with the night before, adding more to it little by little till it was finished. It may not be very good in the eyes of others, but I felt that God was pleased with it, and that was all that mattered, because I had written it for him. And once I finished it, I dedicated it to the Lord as a way of worshiping him and to show him how grateful I was. I called the poem "Becoming a Child in the Lord's Arms," and it reads like this.

> As I look back on my life of fifty-three years, I see mainly sadness, frustration, and tears.
>
> I spent a lifetime searching for the true meaning of love. And ten years ago, I found out that it only comes from above.
>
> One early morning, when I felt like I didn't want to go on, for my will to fight was now gone.
>
> I cried out to the Lord and said "I don't think I can." But I knew in my heart that if anyone could help me, it was the Lord, the great I Am.
>
> I came to the Lord with a heart all broken and torn. And soon come to realize that with Jesus I could be reborn.
>
> Because just moments before, I had felt burdens of sadness and grief, and they had now been lifted and replaced with joy and sighs of relief.
>
> The Lord became my Shepherd on that early summer day. Somehow I knew he would never leave me, and I would never stray.
>
> Each day I will praise him, whether my life is good or full of despair. For I now know in my heart that he will always be there.

He has shown me that I am his child that he holds in the palm of his hands, and nothing can come near me unless he says it can.

So to you I will give the glory my God most high, for helping and preparing me to meet you in the sky.

Many times I have heard people say that they didn't believe the Bible because it was written by men. Well, I can say that I believe what I have read in the Bible because I now know that God's Word is the truth and have seen firsthand his faithfulness to do what his word says on many occasions. For instance, Philippians 4:13, "I can do everything through him who gives me strength." I knew that it wasn't because of my capabilities that I was able to write this poem, but it was because God had given me the words to put on paper.

February would come, and God's blessings would continue. He always seems to show up whenever we need him the most. For some time now, it seemed like when we scheduled the ladies' Bible study, the only ones that would show up was Sue and I. On occasion we might have one or two more that might be there, but most of the time it was just the two of us. I could not help but feel really bad for Sue because I saw that she had a lot on her plate. She worked a full-time job, took care of the children's department at church, taught a Sunday school class, and she was preparing for a Bible study class that no one showed up for but me. All of this left her with very little personal time to do what she needed to do for her or her family. But at the same

THE VISION

time, I realized that she did this because of her love for the Lord.

On one particular night, there were only three of us that showed up. By this time, we were beginning to wonder if we should continue our class or not, so we didn't even attempt to study God's Word. We just decided to spend some time praying, asking God to show us what he wanted. The three of us that were there had said that we didn't want to stop meeting, but we decided to do whatever God led us to do. In the days ahead, I spent a lot of time in prayer because I had seen what God had done in my life, and I couldn't help but think others could benefit as well from the Bible study. But it was now time to lay my will down and allow God's will to be done. I think we had all come to this same conclusion by this time.

After a few days of praying, I felt like God gave me his answer in his Word. It was while I was reading 2 Timothy 3:16–17 that I began to feel like God wanted us to continue our class. Because it said, "All scripture is God-breathed and is useful for teaching, rebuking, correcting and training in righteousness, so that the man of God may be thoroughly equipped for every good work." And as I continued to read in chapter 4 verse 2, it said, "Preach the word; be prepared in season and out of season; correct, rebuke, and encourage with great patience and careful instruction." I was so excited because God let me know in my heart that he wanted us to continue. I couldn't wait to call Sue and hear what God was telling her. After I had shared with her what

God had showed me, she said she felt that God was telling her to continue as well.

 The day of our next meeting was approaching, and Sue had made up some flyers and passed them out at church inviting the ladies to come and join us. But I felt that there was more God wanted us to do. I just didn't know what it was at the time. So I ended up going back to him in prayer asking him to show us. The Sunday before we were scheduled to meet, I felt very strongly that he wanted us to share with the ladies what he had showed me in the Scriptures. And since Sue was the teacher, I felt she should be the one to share this, but God had a different plan. Brother Michael was the one conducting our evening service on that day. And all during that time I felt as if someone was trying to push me out of the pew. By the end of the service, I couldn't sit there any longer, so I asked to speak to the ladies of the church. I felt God's presence, and it seemed like the words I spoke were not my own but the Lord's. It was almost like he was using me to extend a personal invitation to all the ladies that were there. To this day, I cannot remember what it was that I said exactly, but whatever I said seemed to come out very easily, and this was unusual for me.

 I continued to pray for the next two days asking God to work in the hearts of the ladies of the church and bring them to our class on Tuesday night. On Tuesday morning, while I was spending time in prayer and reading the Bible, I would hear God speak to me again. This time I had just finished reading Matthew 22 and the parable of the wedding banquet. When I got to verse 14, it said, "For many are invited, but few are chosen." And that is when I heard the Lord say, "It doesn't matter if there are a lot or a few showing up tonight. Because the ones who are there are my chosen. Just like the twelve disciples I chose." And immediately I was reminded of how blessed they were because they were with Jesus and he was with them. I was so excited because God had said that whoever were there that night were the ones he had chosen. And out of that excitement, I asked him if we could have twelve ladies show up that night.

Well, when I arrived a little after six, I saw new faces that had never been there before, and I saw the excitement on Sue's face that I had been feeling all day. I saw that night an example of how God's love for us will bless us with more than we ever asked for, because I had asked for twelve ladies and we ended up with fourteen for our Bible study. The Word tells us that we need to encourage others, but God is the master when it comes to encouraging. We were ready to give up, but God being the one who can do all things moved in the hearts of the ladies, and they came. And for us who had tried all we knew to do and had become discouraged found ourselves overflowing with joy once again. And because of that joy, we were then encouraged to continue doing what God wanted, and that was spend more time with him in his Word through the ladies' Bible study.

The last two months I experienced blessings on top of blessings and was feeling pretty good because of it. But then March would come, and I would find out that my dad had been seeing doctors concerning a knot on his throat. On March 16 we were going to the VA hospital in Muskogee for a biopsy. And on March 19 we would find out that he had tongue cancer, and it was in stage 4. Things were not looking to good at this point, and I couldn't help but remember what we had experienced in the past. And because it was cancer, and because the memories were not that pleasant, I found myself going to God and asking, "Why are you making us go through this again?" I felt like God immediately began to ask me the same thing he asked the disciples when they found themselves in a boat that was about to sink in a storm, and that was, "Why are you so afraid? Do you still have no faith?" (Mark 4:40). After all that I had seen Jesus do, I realized that I should not let this bother me, but I did. Now the question I was faced with is why. If it had not been for God's words that I had been reading in the Bible and had inside me, I would have never understood. But God did help me understand that the reason we all seem to react in this way is because we do not want the storms to come, and when they do, we want them to stop as soon as possible because none of us like to endure pain, sorrow, or suffering, and we all have a little bit of fear dwelling inside us because of what we have seen, heard, or experienced. It is the fear of the unknown that causes us to focus more on the storm, rather than on the one who can calm the storm, and that is Jesus, who can do all things (Luke 1:37). Even though I had already seen what Jesus could do, when I heard that my dad had stage 4 cancer, based on what I had experienced and what my mother experienced, I began to fear because that is what my life had taught me to do. But then I began to remember the scriptures that said God did not give us a spirit of fear (2 Timothy 1:7), and remembering what God had already taught me, I begin to put two and two together and saw more clearly that it was Satan who was causing me to fear. He was using my circumstances to accomplish it. Now I was in a position to where I needed to choose. Did I believe the lies of Satan, or was I going to believe in Jesus knowing that he does not lie and that nothing was impossible with him? I chose to believe in Jesus and came to realize that sometimes God asks us to endure storms we go through so that he can help someone else. They're not always all about us. I believe that's what he was doing in this case with my dad.

When we found out that my dad had cancer, things started moving at a really fast pace. Before we had time to process what we had been told, the doctors had him scheduled to start treatments. My dad did not understand what the seven weeks of radiation and the three very strong chemo treatments were going to do to his body or his health, even though the doctors were trying to explain it to him, and there wasn't time to help him understand. I did understand all that the doctors were saying because I had experienced it when I had my cancer, and I knew that the road ahead of us was going to be long and hard. But my dad had it in his head that nothing was going to change and he would be able to go on doing all the things he had been doing in the past. I think that God saw we were not ready to start our journey down this road and allowed what would happen in the days to come to slow things down a little so he could help us get ready.

Just a few days before my dad would start his treatments, on March 22, I had a massive heart attack. I had been having some issues whenever I would eat or drink anything, but I thought it was just due to acid reflex. But on this Monday night, Freddy and I went out to eat, and by the time we started home, I felt like my stomach would literally explode. I remember commenting to Freddy about how miserable I felt. I was also experiencing some pain in my left arm, but I figured it was just caused from all the pressure that had built up in my stomach. Shortly after we arrived home, all I wanted to do was go to bed and lie flat so I could relieve that pressure. I remember saying a prayer, and I fell asleep. But a little before midnight, I was awake again, needing to go to the bathroom. As I got up and made my way to the end of the bed, I began to feel like I was going to pass out and knew something was seriously wrong. But the urge to go caused me to continue. By the time I made it to the bathroom door, I knew that I was fixing to black out, and I could not stop it. As I began to fall, I felt my eyes close, and I began to feel the presence of someone at my head and another at my feet. The one at my head placed their arms under my arms and the one at my feet took hold of them. They lay me down on the floor as gentle as you would a baby. Again the first thing I remembered was God's Word in Psalms 91:11–12 that says, "He will command his angels concerning you to guard you in all your ways;

they will lift you up in their hands, so that you will not strike your foot against a stone." Even though I was out of it physically, I knew what was going on. I knew God was with me, and he had sent his angels to protect me. I couldn't move or open my eyes, and because I felt paralyzed all over, I started to think that I had a stroke. I could hear Freddy and others that had arrived rushing around and talking, but when they tried to get me to talk to them, all I could do was lie there. Because of what I was hearing, I knew that things were pretty serious, and I just remember praying asking God to be with my family if something happened to me. Shortly after I got to the hospital, I was completely out of it and didn't know anything until the next morning. And it wasn't until I woke up the next morning did I realize that it was by the grace of God that I was even still here. I was told at that time that the doctors had said that the type of heart attack that I had was what they refer to as the widow maker. The main artery to my heart was 100 percent blocked.

For years I had made myself believe that no one cared anything about me, that I wasn't important to anyone, so there was no reason to even be around. But when I woke up that Tuesday morning and looked around my hospital room and saw all my family anxiously waiting for me to wake up, I realized that this was God's way of showing me that all the things I believed in the past were a lie, and again I saw more clearly just how blessed I was. God had already confirmed to me his love by the things I was seeing him do and through the vision. He was now confirming the love of others in my life, and by allowing me to see their love for me, he helped me regain a little more of the confidence and self-worth my past had taken away.

By Wednesday there had been a lot of people come and go, and my dad was one of them. He had stopped by to let me know that he was going to a small town just south of Tulsa to see his girlfriend at the time. Since we had found out about the cancer, I had been keeping pretty close tabs on him, and he didn't want me to worry since I just had a heart attack. But later that evening we would get a call telling us that he had a heart attack as well and was being rushed back to Tulsa in a helicopter. He wasn't being brought to the same hospital I was in, so I couldn't be there when he arrived. All I could do was pray for him and ask God to take care of him, and he did. By Thursday I had talked my doctor into releasing me so I could go and see for myself that my dad was okay. By Friday he would be released. But for the next month, we couldn't do much of anything. It was a time to just take it easy and recover from our heart attacks. Before this happened, things were moving so fast we didn't have time to think. But now God had definitely slowed things down, and we now had the time we needed to prepare for my dad's treatments.

By the beginning of May, my emotions and feelings was up one minute and down another. With everything that I had experienced since the first of the year, the worry and concern over our finances, my dad's cancer and both of us having a heart attack, and the concerns I had because of the treatments, I just felt like I needed someone to talk to that would understand. And that someone happened to be God. I knew in my heart that everything would be okay, but I needed him to confirm it by allowing me to feel his presence and maybe hear a word from him that would encourage me and eliminate the fear that was trying to arise in me. So I was spending a lot of time in prayer. I knew the next several months were not going to be easy for any of us.

Well, I would hear a word from the Lord, but it wasn't what I was expecting and wasn't what I wanted to hear. A week before my dad was to start his treatments, I was reading in the Bible in Luke 22. And when I got to verses 31 and 32, I saw the words rise up higher than all the other words on the page. It was almost like they were jumping off the page at me. Based on my past experiences with the Lord, I knew in my heart he was trying to get me to pay attention. I just felt like he was saying, "Take note, pay attention, this is for you." As I continued to read, it said, "Simon, Simon, Satan has asked to sift you as wheat." And I felt like the Lord replaced Simon's name with mine. But then it went on to say, "But I have prayed for you, Simon, that your faith may not fail. And when you have turned back, strengthen your brother." I continued to read these same two verses over and over, asking the Lord, "Are you telling me that this is what I can expect?" And before I closed my Bible, I had become pretty concerned. If what had just happened was truly God speaking to me and Satan had asked to sift me as wheat. I knew there was no telling what he was going to do in my life. And I wasn't sure I wanted to find out. I couldn't help but recall the story of Job in the Bible and what happened to him when Satan asked to sift him as wheat. And I knew there was no way I wanted to experience what he did. But aside from feeling a little afraid, I also found myself feeling a little bit of encouragement because in Job's situation God restored all that Satan had taken away in the end, and in the scriptures I had just read it showed me that the Lord was with me and praying for me, and he would see me through for it said, "When you have turned back, strengthen your brother." This meant I would have to get through whatever I would have to face; otherwise, the Lord would not be able to use me to help someone else.

I believe that I am no different than anyone. I don't like it when I have to face difficult times. But I have learned through all these experiences and have come to accept a very important fact about life, God did not promise that we wouldn't see difficult times, but he did promise that he would never leave us or forsake us during those times (Hebrews 13:5). And I believe that is what the Lord wanted me to see when he showed me the vision and connected it to Psalms 23. By using the vision, Psalms 23, along with what he was doing, he could develop my faith. And it would rise to a level that when I faced the valleys I would encounter, I could say with my mouth and know in my heart that because God was with me, I did not have to fear the unknown because the Bible tells us, "Greater is He that is in you than he that is in the world" (1 John 4:4).

By the beginning of June, my dad had been through ten of the radiation and one of his chemo treatments, and the side effects from them were really starting to kick in. On June 2, we found ourselves returning to the VA hospital in Muskogee so the doctors could put a feeding tube in. It had gotten harder for him to swallow, and he was beginning to lose a lot of weight. Over the next month, I spent a lot of time in prayer because we were in and out of the hospital a lot. My dad did not accept the feeding tube very well because he was a very proud man, and he felt embarrassed to think that he had to have assistance to be able to eat. So he refused to allow me to feed him through the tube, and this caused all kinds of problems. There was a time when he wasn't able to talk, and this made it hard to communicate with him, so we had to deal with his frustration and ours. There were even times that we didn't know if he would make it or not. But I kept holding on to the hope that I had found in God's Word and continued to go to him in prayer asking for his help. The church had added him to our prayer list, so I had comfort in knowing that others were praying for him as well. Even though Freddy and I were experiencing a little fatigue during this time, we found the strength to continue to do what needed to be done through our time spent with the Lord. And I knew that this is what God wanted me to do. By this time, I was beginning to understand that he would not ask me to do something unless he planned on giving me the means and ability to do it.

On June 29, my dad's sister and I took him in for his last chemo and radiation treatment. I was so glad to see that day come. The last few months we had experienced a lot of ups and downs. But now that the treatments were finished, I felt my dad had a greater chance for recovery. But it was now time to wait and see if the treatments had been successful in getting rid of the cancer. Our time of waiting over the next three months wasn't very easy because we were all anxious to see if the cancer was gone. And we knew that if it wasn't gone, the more time that passed, the more time it gave the cancer to grow again.

 Well, by the first week of October, we were finally on our way to get the results of his PET scan. He had an appointment to see his chemo oncologist first, and then we were scheduled to see the ENT specialist. We sat there in the oncologist's office with high expectations. He began by telling us that the PET scan had showed that the cancer was still there and was worse than before he started. I couldn't believe what I was hearing. I felt like my heart had dropped to my feet. I could tell that my dad and his sister June was feeling the same way by the look on their faces. And I begin to question the doctor's findings by saying, "How can that be? His blood work had come back normal, he was gaining weight, and he was feeling better than I had seen him feel for a very long time. And then I asked, "Aren't these all signs that the cancer is gone?" And he replied by saying, "I know everything else is saying that the cancer is gone, but the PET scan says it is worse." And he immediately told my dad that he wanted him to start taking another round of chemo treatments, and this time they would have to be stronger than before. I had felt for a while now that God had healed my dad, but this doctor was trying to tell me that he hadn't and

The Vision

wanted to put him through more chemo that I didn't feel he needed. And because his body was already to the point of not being able to handle anything else, I didn't feel he could survive another bout with chemo.

We were all feeling angry, sad, disappointed, and confused when we left his office and went to meet with the ENT specialist. We didn't have much to say to him at first. I guess because we wanted to hear what his thought was without being influenced by the oncologist's report. After he had put a scope down my dad's throat to get a visual look of things, he said to us that he did not see any cancer, only the repercussion from the radiation treatments. Now we were really confused. We had two different reports, one good and one bad, and we were thinking to ourselves, *Which one is true?* After talking with the ENT doctor some more, we left his office believing his report and not the oncologist's. It just seemed to make more sense. So we returned to the oncologist to share with that doctor the ENT's findings. But he had already made up his mind that he indeed had cancer and needed to start chemo treatments again right away.

As we were leaving the hospital, I began to feel as though God was speaking to me trying to help me understand what had just happened. I felt he said, "You believed that I had healed your dad and Satan knew that. He used the oncologist to try and get you to doubt. But I used the ENT specialist to confirm to you that what you believed was true. You now have to choose which one you will believe. Continue to have faith and believe in me and you will see my glory revealed." After talking to my dad and trying to help him understand what the doctors were telling us, I was so glad to hear him say that he wanted to get a second opinion. I knew this would mean we would have to wait even longer before we would know for sure if he was cancer free, and waiting has never been something I was very good at.

I now know that the reason God ask us to wait and be patient sometimes is because it can mean the difference between whether we will experience the life of something or the death of something, blessing or curses, and he gives us the freedom to choose which one it will be (Deuteronomy 30:19). He has helped me see that he gave us the freedom to choose so we would not be controlled by anyone else and become their slave. And when we are free to choose what we do, how we think, where we go, and we don't make the right choose, then we have to understand that it is our fault no one else's. But I have learned from my own experiences that unless we have all the facts, like knowing the truth, what God says about the situation, we cannot have discernment between what God would have us to do or what Satan wants. And we will choose based on what we know and what we can see, and we will choose the death of something almost every time. If I had not known about God and what he could do, out of the fear of the cancer and what it could possibly do to my dad, I probably would have suggested that he do what the oncologist said. And that would have been the wrong choice in our situation.

I was beginning to feel really tired and a little stressed out because of what we had experienced so far this year. And because of how I was feeling, it was really hard to handle the fact that Freddy's work had begun to slow down again. We were only two months away from Christmas by this time, and the thought of not being able to buy some little something for my daughter and granddaughters was really upsetting. Always before God had provided what we needed, but this year seemed to be different. It was almost like he was purposely holding back, and I didn't understand why. So I spent more time in prayer asking him to show me. Before long I felt God's spirit speaking to me, and he began to help me to see that in almost every area of my life he had been making changes that were good and helping us to move forward. But even though we were making progress in eliminating some of our debt, we were not changing anything that we were doing concerning our finances. And this was causing us to go around that same old mountain each year. Then he reminded me of the prayer I had been praying for some time asking him to help us so that we wouldn't have to go around that same old mountain. And he let me know that before he could help me, I had to start doing my part, and I felt God's reprimand very strongly. It was like he was telling me, "If what you have been doing for years isn't working for you, then it is time to make some changes. And if you are not willing to make those changes, then stop complaining to me when you find yourself going around that mountain." He had once told me while I was praying and asking for his help, "You have been treading water long enough, either you start swimming, or you are going to drown." In other words, make the changes in what you are doing.

I couldn't see it at the time, but I was still viewing money the same way the world does, and during this time, God was trying to get me to see that, and let me know that I had not yet learned how to be content in all situations. In my time of reflecting back, I began to see that I wasn't content with what I did have in our time of lack, and God was trying to teach me, because without contentment, there could not be any peace in my life.

By using his Word and my everyday experiences, God began to help me make those changes that needed to take place and change my attitude about money a little more. He helped me see that I had been doing the same thing the Israelites were doing while they were in the desert after he had delivered them from bondage. He had made them a promise that he was going to lead them to the promised land. But when things got hard or were not the way they thought they should be, they went to Moses and griped and complained, forgetting the promise he had made them and not thanking him for what he had already done. God reminded me of how I had been telling him how grateful I was, but every winter I was coming to him griping and complaining about what we were going through. And he wanted me to know that gratitude is not shown by grumbling and complaining, and that is what I was doing in my time of lack. Through my experiences, God was able to show me how I allowed my circumstances concerning my money to control my thoughts and my feelings once

THE VISION

again. And each time that happened, I lost sight of the vision and the assurance and promise that come along with it and would lose my contentment and peace.

Paul wrote in Philippians 4:12–13, "I have learned the secret of being content in any and every situation, whether well fed or hungry, whether living in plenty or in want." But I was beginning to see that before we can learn this, we have to experience all those things first, just as I believed God allowed Paul to. And I would soon come to realize that what God did with Paul, he was now going to do with me.

In the month of December, God provided just enough work for Freddy so that we could pay the bills that had to be paid. We had just enough left over so I could buy a little something for our daughter and granddaughters. He would also give us the best Christmas present we could ever receive, and that was we found out that my dad was now cancer free. I believe that he knew Freddy and I would be facing the worst winter ever financially, and he encouraged us with this good news about my dad, but he also gave us hope through other things we would hear about for the days ahead.

Two weeks before Christmas, I would get a call from my aunt telling me that my brother, sister, and I may be entitled to royalties off gas wells that was on some property our grandfather had owned. And she gave me the number to the attorneys that was handling things. I couldn't help but think that this might be another way God was going to help us turn that curve financially. It wasn't something that would help us out in our present time, but it might be something that would help us out in our future. And that gave me hope, and when we have hope, then we have something to look forward to, and it makes it easier to endure the hardships we may encounter along the way. I was seeing that just as God used Jesus to give us who believe in him hope for a better life with him in heaven. Through his grace in our lives and our experiences here on Earth, he gives us hope for a better life here and now. But we have to choose to see and hold on to his grace and not let Satan's attacks blind us to what God is doing. And we do that by allowing God to be a part of our life and constantly renewing our mind by spending time reading or hearing his words. For it tells us in Romans 12:2, "Do not conform any longer to the pattern of this world, but be transformed by the renewing of your mind. Then you will be able to test and approve what God's will is—his good, pleasing and perfect will."

January and February Freddy was without work again. God had showed me what the problems were in my life back in December. It was now time to see if I had learned anything and was willing to do what needed to be done. We were living on about fifty dollars a week by this time. And to be honest, I don't understand how he did it, but if it had not been for God making it stretch, I don't think we would have been able to manage. Out of the fifty dollars we were able to buy just enough gas so that we could continue going over to my dad's. Because he still needed our help as he recovered, and we continued to go to church. And we managed to buy just enough groceries to get by. No, we were not eating steaks every night, but we were eating. Our financial situation had been bad in the past but never as bad as this.

By the end of February, we had found ourselves two months behind on our house payment, and four months behind on Freddy's truck that he used for work. Our utilities and phone were going to be shut off in a couple of days. It was the middle of winter, and I knew that if things didn't change quickly we were going to be without heat or even a place to live. I wasn't able to go to work at the time because I was spending all my time taking care of my dad. Not knowing what to do, I found myself going back to the Lord, asking him to show me what it was we could do. Almost immediately the thought of selling my mother's rings and the ring Freddy had bought me just a few years earlier came to me. But I will say I struggled with that thought because of the sentimental attachment I had toward them both, and that made it harder to let go of either one. But I couldn't help but remember Job again. He had lost all that was important to him, but because he did not turn his back on God and give up on what he believed, the Lord restored all that Satan had taken away from him and more. And then God reminded me of the time he spoke to me about Jacob and Benjamin, where he said, "As long as Jacob held on to Benjamin he only received baskets full of provision. It was only after he decided to give up his Benjamin, that he started to receive wagons full of what he needed" (Genesis chapters 42–45), and then he asked me again, "What is your Benjamin that you are holding on to?" That is when I was able to see that I had made the rings my Benjamin.

Many times over the last ten years, God has had to remind me that I am holding on to things that in the end really won't matter. And without realizing it, I made those things my god. God reopened my eyes that had become blinded, and with his help, I was able to get back on track with my thinking. And I began to see that sometimes we have to sacrifice today for what we want tomorrow, but that doesn't mean the sacrifice is going to be easy for us. I knew I had to turn my attention back toward God and what he could do so I would not get caught up in what my eyes were seeing. I made the decision to sell the rings.

But right before I would go to Freddy and tell him what I decided to do, God laid upon my heart to call my daughter and ask her if she wanted to buy the rings. At least this would be a way for them to stay in the family, and when we got back on our feet, I could have an opportunity to buy them back. Even though this was an option, it was not the option I wanted to take. I guess you could say I was letting my pride get in the way again. I didn't want our daughter to know just how bad things were for us. I had always felt like children are supposed to be the ones who come to parents for help, not the other way around. But because the feeling was so strong, I laid my pride aside and gave Melissa a call. She refused to buy the rings but insisted on loaning us the money so that we could pay what we had to pay. It was really hard to accept her offer, but at the time, I knew of nothing else we could do. And I strongly felt the Lord telling me to accept. I remember crying all day because we had to go to our daughter for help. But also because I was seeing the Lord provide for our needs when we needed it the most. Again this was not the way I wanted God to provide, but the Scripture tells us in Isaiah 55:8, "For my thoughts are not your thoughts, neither are your ways my ways, "Declares the Lord." Once again I saw that God's way of doing things can be hard for me to accept, but when I choose to do things his way, I did not come away disappointed.

Freddy and I accepted the loan from our daughter and son-in-law. By doing so, we were able to keep our utilities and phone. We were able to get our house payments caught up and make a payment on Freddy's truck. But before we had a chance to talk to the people on the truck and let them know we had made a payment, we had a man show up at our door to repossess it. In the past, I would have become very upset, because without a truck Freddy would have no way to haul the carpet, which meant he couldn't work. But I stayed very calm. In fact I surprised myself at how calm I was. But now I can see that it was because I wasn't focusing on the negative that losing the truck represented. But I was focusing on the good that God was doing in our life and hanging on to the hope he had given me through the vision. Because what I saw through this experience is God not taking something away from us, but he was eliminating some more of our debt, helping us to get closer to turning the curve in our finances. The truck had become more of a burden rather than a blessing, because each month we struggled to pay the payment. And God took away the burden and lightened our load.

I said before, losing the truck, which represents the material things in our life, would have been devastating for us. But over the last ten years, God has helped me to understand that the things we hold on to in our life that we think will bring us happiness are just stuff. And even though it is nice to have it, and in most cases we work hard to get it, and we don't like it when we have to give it up, we can't let our stuff become more important to us than our God. They cannot give us a lasting contentment and peace that we are looking for on the mountaintop, because eventually our stuff that we receive in this world will need to be replaced. But God and the things he brings along with him will last for eternity.

It was at this time that everything that God had taught me and the things I had read out of the Bible started coming together and making more sense. It was like we had been putting a puzzle together piece by piece, and the picture became clearer with each piece that was added. I had now learned the secret of how to be content in any and every situation that Paul talks about in Philippians 4:12, and contentment is a key ingredient to living a life on the mountaintop. I realized that because of the love that God had for me, no matter what he did in my life, his love would never fail to do what was good for me. Again I was reminded that the Bible tells us that "Love never fails" (1 Corinthians 13:8). Through Jesus, all things are possible. For it tells us in Luke 1:37, "For nothing is impossible with God." So therefore I can say with hope, confidence, and expectation, "I can do everything through him who gives me strength" (Philippians 4:13).

And this allows me to focus on the prize at the end of the race rather than on the race itself, just like Paul said he did. But because I am human, which means I am not perfect, who's to say that in the future I may need to be reminded of this when I find myself faced with another problem and lose my contentment. But I believe that because God does love us, if this happens, he will help me find it again.

As I look back at all the things God has taught me by having me live and experience the vision in my life, I can now see that he doesn't just concentrate on one area of our life, but he works in ways that will take care of everything that concerns us, making our life whole and complete, which in turn makes us happy. That is why I have said that he has helped me turn that curve in more ways than one. And since I feel as though I am no longer living in the valley, I think it would be safe for me to say that yes I have turned that curve.

It was while I was watching a movie on TV about a young woman who found herself pregnant and in prison that I heard one of the other inmates quote her a passage out of a book she was reading, which said, "We are all a prisoner until we begin to ask questions." Since God enrolled me in his school, I have learned many lessons, and they have not always been easy. But with every lesson learned, I have gained more wisdom and knowledge that answered the questions in my life that caused me to feel as if I was a prisoner within myself and made me feel as though I had fallen into a valley. I now see that it is the answers to our questions that are the key to setting us free, and it is the wisdom and knowledge that give us the answers. God shows us in Proverbs chapter 3 the many benefits from gaining wisdom. For it says, (v 8) it brings health to our bodies, (v 14) it is more profitable than silver and yields better returns than gold. (v 16) Long life is in her right hand; in her left are riches and honor. (v 17) Her ways are pleasant ways, and all her paths are peace. And In (v 18) Wisdom is a tree of life to those who embrace her; those who lay hold of her will be blessed.

Upon reading this and combining it with what I had seen Jesus do in my life up to this point and time, I realized that God was describing the life on the mountaintop and in Jesus wisdom and knowledge that we need to have this life could be found. Because he is the Word of God, for we are told in John 1:1, "In the beginning was the Word, and the Word was with God, and the Word was God." (v 3) "Through him all things were made;" (v 4) "The Word became flesh and made his dwelling among us." Since Jesus is the Word God was talking about, and if the Word is the wisdom and knowledge that gives us life, it only made sense to me that before I can have a life on the mountaintop that we all want, I had to include him in every area concerning my life. Once I began to understand all of this, it made me even more dedicated to him to choose to pray, read my Bible, and go to church. During those times are when I felt his presence the most.

But there is one more thing that he helped me see and understand, and it was while I attended his school, the church, he was able to help me take my last two steps that would lead me out of the valley. He taught me how to love as though I had never been hurt, which led me to obeying him. I learned by hearing the Word just how much our Heavenly Father loves all of us and all he is willing to do for us because of that love. And through the examples of others in our church, I saw the fruits of love being displayed. Once I become a part of this, that is when I began to experience the joy that comes from love and that caused me to want to love others even more. The more joy we experience, the more we see ourselves becoming content. And contentment is what makes us feel as though we are living on the mountaintop.

This is the reason God commands all of us to love the Lord with all your heart and with all your soul and with all your mind and with all your strength. And love our neighbor as ourselves (Mark 12:30–31). God has showed me that when we choose to obey him, we are no longer just any child. But our actions cause us to become his child in his arms. And then his will will become our will, and we become one, and this allows him to do and fulfill his plans for our life, because we cannot do it by ourselves. And those are found in Jeremiah 29:11, "'For I know the plans I have for you,' declares the Lord, 'plans to prosper you and not to harm you, plans to give you hope and a future.'" I have come to realize that we both wanted the same thing, but in the past, because I was working against him instead of working with him, neither one of us was able to see happen what we wanted to happen. And that is, for me to have a life on the mountaintop, where I could experience a little taste of heaven while here on earth and enjoy my journey as he leads me home.

Retuning to the Valley

I heard my pastor say one time that it only takes a moment to be saved, but it takes a long time to become a disciple God can use. Ten years ago, God let me know that he wanted me to write a book about the vision. But it wasn't until December 2010 did he actually begin to allow me to put anything down on paper. And it just happened to be during a time when Freddy and I were struggling the most with our finances. As I continue to reflect back on my life, I can see how he was using the writing of the book as a way to keep me focused on him rather than on my problems. This was his way of helping me and he continued to teach me what I needed to learn.

When I first began to write down all the things that I had experienced and learned, there was so much to share. I found myself spending all my days and many of my nights writing and was a little overwhelmed by it all. After spending four months writing, I felt like I had finished the book. And I had waited so long to see this day come that when it did finally get here, I found myself feeling anxious to get it published. So I began to contact different companies that might want to publish it for me. I was overcome with excitement when the companies I had submitted the book to responded in a positive way and agreed to publish it. And for the next several months, I spent all of my time trying to make it happen, but I kept running into all kinds of roadblocks. My flesh wanted to hurry and get it into the hands of others, but at the same time, there was something inside me that kept telling me that there was more I was supposed to share and more work needed to be done to it first. I see now that God was in control of things, and by creating roadblocks, he was trying to get me to see that even though I had written the first draft of the book, it still wasn't the way he wanted it to read. And yes I was left feeling a little disappointed because there was a delay in sharing the good news. But I also stayed encouraged because I continued to see God work concerning the book. And this left me knowing in my heart that when the time was right and the book was the way God wanted it to be, he would provide a way for it to get in the hands of others. I knew he had a plan and purpose for it, but in the meantime, he kept telling me that I had more to learn, and so it was back to the classroom.

When I began 2012, I found myself having a desire within me to do more to reach out and help others who were hurting. I began to look for ways I might be able to do just that. For some time, I had been seeing similar signs in the people of our church that I saw in me when I first began this journey. And because I had seen what God could do, I wanted so much to share that good news with them so that they could come out of the valleys they had fallen into and would not have to suffer any longer. I knew what that kind of suffering could do to a person if it did not stop, and I didn't want to see that to happen to any of them when there was no reason for it. By this time, God had made it very clear to me that he did not want any of his children to live in the valleys any longer and that there was a way out. But I was still not sure how or in what way to relay that message.

The desire to share continued to be very strong, and it was driving me to do something. So I finally decided to try and start an outreach program at the church. My thought was, in the midst of helping others with their immediate problems, we could somehow share the vision and message with those who came to us. But I continued to struggle because I had good intentions and the desire, but I had no experience. For years I had been the student, and now God was trying to get me to be the teacher, and it just didn't seem to be working out. All I could think about was how important the vision was and what a difference it could make in the lives of those who were just like me. But at the same time, I couldn't help but feel that in some way I might mess things up because of my inability to speak. Over the years, I had seen how the work of God in me had improved my speech somewhat and was seeing my confidence grow, but the task had not yet been completed. So the fear of failure was still controlling my actions, which was hindering me from doing what God had asked me to do. I had tried once before to teach our Bible study class when Sue was not able to. But I saw very quickly that it is not so easy to do something if you have not learned how to do it first. And once we fail, the fear of failure will normally stop us from trying it again. But as I said before, God teaches us what we need to know by having us live it out, so by our victories and our mistakes, we can see more clearly what needs to be done and remind us we can do nothing without him.

Over time, the more I've seen the desire rise up within me to help others, the more I saw that fear had less control over me. And this is when I confided in Freddy what I felt God wanted me to do concerning the outreach. Together we shared it with our youth minister and his wife, and Michael and Katrina Hartman, who are our associate pastor and his wife. I had seen through the work they were doing in our church that they had a passion for helping people. So I went to them and asked them to pray about the outreach program and see if this might be something they would consider being a part of. After a couple of weeks, they all agreed that this was a good idea, and began to share their concerns for some of the people in the church. They didn't mention anyone by name, but because they knew of their situation, they felt they could benefit from such a program. And because they had all seen such a need, they suggested that it be shared with the people of our church first before we took it outside into the community.

I had begun to feel like God wanted us to share the vision with the church first as well, because the church consisted of people who had already become God's children. But even though God was leading us to share the vision with the church, we continued to try and start the outreach so everyone could hear about it. Over the next few months, nothing we did was able to bring anything about. By this time, God had called our youth minister and his wife away from our church to live and do mission work in Madagascar. And that left Michael, Katrina, Fred, and I, and we all decided to share the vision and its message with the people in the church in a discipleship training class on Sunday evenings. I felt there had to be some kind of lesson to follow that would allow all of us to share the vision and the good news. And a part of me was hoping that with a lesson plan, the others who attended our class would be able to see and understand more clearly, with God's help, what God had showed me. I spent most of the summer trying to put it all down on paper, and I can say that in no way was it professionally done. But God was able to use it to help me grow and helped me see what it was I was supposed to share. By the end of July, I had come up with what I thought might work, and we shared with the church our plans to start this new discipleship training class in August. I had said that I felt that a lesson plan was important so all of us would be equally involved and share in the teaching. But the truth of the matter is, I was hoping that with having a lesson to follow, the others could do most of the talking, and I would speak only to fill in the blanks, and this would cut down the chances of me messing things up. But again God had a different plan. Because it was I who had seen the vision and had experienced it, it seemed like I was the one doing most of the teaching in our class. I knew in my heart that this was God's way of helping me to overcome my insecurities, and gain the experience I needed, and continued to teach me what I needed to learn, but it didn't make it any easier, and I will say there was a lot of mistakes made.

Well, I did learn a lot with this experience and began to see what I was sharing that wasn't so important and important things that I had left out. Without me realizing it at the time, God was using this study and the people to fine-tune how he would have me share the vision with others in the book. But I will say that upon seeing the mistakes that I had made, I was left feeling as though I had let the Lord down, as well as all the people who come to our training class. And I ended the class thinking that if it had been done by someone else, it would have turned out a lot better. And I remember praying telling God just how sorry I was for not accomplishing what I felt he wanted me to do. And because of how I was feeling I decided at this time that I didn't want to have anything else to do with sharing the vision with anyone and the only way I would even consider it is if God showed me specifically what he wanted me to do step by step. I have since learned this attitude is not acceptable to God. But I remember going home and taking all my notes and everything that I had accumulated over the years that had anything to do with the vision or the book. I put it in a box and put it away.

But just a few weeks after we had finished our discipleship training class that we called "Turning Valleys into Mountaintops," the urge to work on the book came back. But even though I felt this strong urge, I couldn't bring myself to do anything. I saw myself going back in time feeling like a failure, and this was not where I wanted to be. It seemed like I was in the middle of a battle again. And the reason was because I was putting more focus on myself and what I had done, instead of God and what he was doing in me. It wasn't long before I began to see my feelings of being a failure fighting against the urges that God placed inside me, and for the next few weeks, I did all that I could so I wouldn't think about the vision or the book. And when a thought did try to appear, I worked even harder to diminish that thought.

Many times since I had started reading the Bible I found myself relating to Moses. And I don't say that because I see myself like Moses but because of my inability to speak with clarity just like Moses said he was. On many occasions I felt like saying to God the same as he did, "Who am I Lord?" (Exodus 3:11). My thoughts were, "Lord, I have trouble talking, how can you ask me to tell others about the vision, when you know I will only mess things up because my words never come out the way they are supposed to?" And the fact that I had just had an experience where I felt like I had failed in doing what God wanted made these feelings I was having even more intense. So working on the book that was about the vision was the last thing that I wanted to do. But God continued to be in control of the situation because he put an even stronger desire within me to share the good news. And at the same time he was working in me to get me back on track with how I was thinking. He did all of this by reminding me of what he told Moses in Exodus 4:11–12. The scriptures tell us that Moses tried to make excuses and told God that he was slow in his speech and tongue, and he asked him to send someone else to speak to Pharaoh. God replied by saying, "Who gave man his mouth? Who makes him deaf or mute? Who gives sight or makes him blind? Is it not I, the Lord? Now go; I will help you speak and will teach you what to say." It was through his Holy Spirit and the scriptures that he reminded me that the success of the book or what he could do in the lives of others because of the vision had nothing to do with me and what I could do. Its purpose and his plan was to show me and others what he could do and show that he was Lord.

 I have seen in my own life just how easy it is to make everything about us if we are not careful. But I have also seen that when we have the Lord with us, he is quick to get our focus back on him and set us straight. He knows just how to keep us humble and keep us on that highway. God did cause me to become humble before him again, and I picked up the book and started working on it shortly after we finished with our class in 2013. And just like the first time, I couldn't seem to leave it alone. Many times I would be sitting at my kitchen table working on it when my husband left for work, and I would still be there in the evening when he returned. During this time, I couldn't help but feel

THE VISION

a little a shamed because nothing else was being done. But I knew in my heart this was something that I had to do, so everything else had to be put on hold.

As I began to write, it was like the words just kept coming. And this time I felt in my heart that they were the way God wanted them to read. And it was while I was rewriting the book that God was able to help me see the missing link to the vision that I had failed to see that would make the vision and its message that it contains complete. And I also think it was his way of completing the fence that would keep me from ever falling off the mountain again, where he had placed me.

Even after all this time and all that I had seen God do in my life, I was still trying to turn that curve and become debt free by what I was doing and the way the world would, instead of relying on God totally to help me to do it. So I saw my peace of mind that he wanted me to have come and go constantly. One minute I was on top of the mountain, and the next I felt like I was in the valley again. I guess you could say, in a lot of ways, I was still trying to live my life with one foot in the world and one on the highway, trying to experience the very best of both. God had said before that when I turned that curve I would be debt free. But what he said to me this time was "All your debts have been paid in full. Because when you accepted Jesus as your Lord, what he had done already, long before you we're ever born, paid them off for you on that day." What he needed for me to see is that because of Jesus nothing that I could ever want, need, or even desire was not impossible to have. Because he was sent to us to represent all things that we are in need of so that through him we could have the life that he hoped we would have. And through him all things are made possible so I didn't have to work so hard to become debt free, because in the end, nothing I could do would make it happen unless he made it happen." I realized in that moment that to be the child in the Lord's arms, where he wanted me to be, I had to rely on him totally just like a newborn baby would its mother. Not in some ways, but all ways, not sometimes, but all the time. And for someone who is now fifty-six years old, that is easier said than done. Maybe that is the reason it has taken so long to bring it about. But with God's help, I am seeing myself doing it more and more.

Upon hearing what he had said to me, I immediately remembered what I had read in his Word in Deuteronomy 8:18, "But remember the Lord your God, for it is He that gives you the ability to produce wealth." Once again he had to remind me, "You are nothing and can do nothing without me." It became more clear to me that it is God's presence and his constant reminders through the things we will see him do that keeps us on that highway, and keeps our faith strong so we can do what seems almost impossible. When he told me that all my debts had been paid in full, if I had not had this wisdom and knowledge and faith in place where I could believe in things not yet seen, I would have doubted or questioned what God had said to me on that day, because the world and my circumstances were still telling me that I had debts that needed to be paid. But he helped me see that through Jesus even those could be taken care of, and this gave me the hope to live with that caused me to expect to see that I would be debt free in this world one day. It is this type of faith that causes us to begin to live and act as his child in his arms in this world and gives us the ability to trust, wait, and be patient as God works everything out no matter how long it may take. Because when you can believe in things not yet seen, there is no reason for questions or fear, and then Satan has nothing that he can use to manipulate or control you with. And even though he continues to attack, he cannot rob you of your peace, joy, and happiness that God wants us to have as we make our way in this life because of the hope we have found in the Lord. I have learned that it is this type of faith that causes us to become confident in what we believe, and this pleases God, because it does take away Satan's control over us and opens the door that will allow Jesus to come in and work the miracle signs and wonders in our lives that the Bible talks about so that others will see that he is Lord.

I think a part of me knew all this in my heart from all that I had seen God do in my life over the last several years and from reading the Bible. But I was still having trouble putting it into words so I could share it with others. And sometimes we have to experience one of those aha moments before we begin to see things clearly as they really are.

I have shared already how Satan uses the negative things we have stored in our mind to keep us in the valleys in his attempt to destroy us. These are the things we have seen through our eyes of the flesh and will keep us spiritually blinded to the things of God. And

I believe that is what Paul is talking about when he tells us in 2 Corinthians 4:4, "The god of this age has blinded the minds of unbelievers, so that they cannot see the glory of Christ, who is the image of God." But when God spoke to me and told me that my debts had been paid in full, I saw in that moment how he took the wisdom and knowledge of him and what he could do that he had put in place instead of the negative things in my mind, and allowed me to begin to see things through the eyes of my spirit. It is when we begin to see things through the eyes of the spirit that we find the faith to believe and trust in the one taking care of us. And we are able to do as Paul said he did, and that is focus on the prize at the end of race and not on the race itself.

I have come to understand with God's help that our life and the things we experience in this world we live in today is the race. And the prize is God's promises in the Bible as we run the race as well as our eternal home once the race is finished. The reason that I say this is because God has allowed me to see that the kingdom of heaven comes in two stages, the here and now and the future. The future kingdom of heaven is a gift from God, and it is a place where everything has already been made perfect. And the only requirement to receive his gift is to believe and call on the name of the Lord Jesus, God's Son. But the kingdom of heaven of the here and now is not so perfect because it is full of our sin, which causes holes and cracks in our life. And even though God does not like our sin, he does like our holes and cracks because through Jesus, it is possible for his light, his glory, to shine through for all to see. But he has helped me to understand that before his light can shine and we can experience the kingdom of heaven of the here and now, we are required to have faith and fulfill our covenant agreement that we have made with him. And that is, we have to allow Jesus to be Lord of our life while we are living here. Giving him control so that he can fulfill God's will for us because we cannot do it on our own because of the sin in us. That is why Jesus said in John 10:10, "I have come so that they may have life, and have it to the full." The key word in this phrase being *may*. This means God has already provided a place for us on the mountain, but that doesn't mean everyone will experience it because not everyone is willing to do their part to fulfill the covenant agreement to receive it.

Jesus tells us in Luke 18:27, "What is impossible with men is possible with God." Time after time I have seen God take what seemed like an impossible situation in my life and make it possible. And because of this, I have found the hope that I have in God today, and it has brought me and inner peace, joy, and happiness, and allowed me to dream and make plans for the future. And even though I know in my heart I may never see some of the things I hope for come about in this life, I now know that what I hope for could come about when God is involved. And this allows me to live a life of expectation, expecting to see something good happen every day even though I still live in this world where evil lurks around every corner.

When God first began to teach me the things about him and his ways, I did not always understand, because it seemed to me as though everything was being turned upside down or backward from what I had learned up to this point. But because God always finishes what he starts, he used the time we had together and had the patience with me until he could help me understand. And when the wisdom and knowledge of him had been put in place inside me and the time was right, he used something as simple as working a puzzle to bring about this understanding and make it clear in my mind that I would like to share now.

It was after I had worked on putting a puzzle together and had come down to the last few pieces and couldn't make them fit anywhere that I realized I had made a mistake and had to go back and try to find what piece I had put in the wrong place before the puzzle could be completed. God took all that I had experienced and learned over the years to bring everything together, and opened my eyes to see, that just like I had the desire and bought the puzzle I was working because of the picture I saw on the box. I had this desire to have this life on the mountaintop because of the picture he had placed inside me. He is the creator of life's puzzle. And he places this picture of this type of life in each person because of his love for us, and this is his hope for all of us his children.

He showed me that just like the manufacturer created the picture of the puzzle I was working, they also created the order in which it was to be put together. And they did that by taking the whole picture and cutting it into many pieces. Knowing that as the individual connected each piece together in the order it was designed to be connected, they would see the picture being revealed right before their eyes. And that is what God did with our life's puzzle. He did not present it to us already worked but in pieces, designed to be put together piece by piece as we grow and mature, therefore creating and order in which our life was to be lived out. And by giving us the freedom to choose, it was his way of allowing us the opportunity to work the puzzle for ourselves, giving us back the power and control the way he intended it to be before the fall of the first man he created (Genesis 1:28–30).

By comparing the puzzle I was working, with the puzzle of life, he allowed me to see that when we try to live our life the way the world tells us to, what we are doing is putting pieces to the puzzle he has created for us in the wrong places. Because this world represents sin and sin is what blinds us to the things of God. And this causes us to never be able to experience the fullness of life that he had hoped that we would have because the puzzle cannot be completed in the end. Therefore, we will experience the valleys. But not only does it stop us from having the life that God wanted for us, and take away our power and control that God intended for us to have, but it makes us vulnerable to become someone else's slaves. And because we live in a sinful world and Satan is the father of sin, he becomes the slave master over us. Always prompting us to go where he wants us to go, and doing what he wants us to do, so that he can fulfill his purpose. And that is to steal, kill, and destroy us. This causes us to put the wrong pieces of the puzzle in the wrong places.

I would not have been able to see and understand all of this if it had not been for Jesus. Because this is not something that can be seen through the eyes of our flesh, nor have we been taught in this world, but this is something that can only be see through the eyes of our spirit. And God showed me that he created us with both. He gave us the eyes of the flesh so we could see to make our way through this world, but in many places in the scriptures, he warns that we should not become like the ones in this world. And he gave us the eyes of the spirit so we could continue to see and remember him and find our way back home when the time was right. But because we live in a sinful world where there is more evil being done than good, the sin blinds our spiritual eyes. And before long we see less and less of God and what he represents and our life will become unbalanced. And when this happens, we tend to see more and focus more on the bad things that are happening in our lives and this will make us feel as though we are in and out of the valleys constantly. That is why he says in the Bible that we have eyes but do not see and ears to hear but do not hear (Ezekiel 12:2).

Before I began this journey, I could only see all the bad things going on in my life. The bad I saw cause my thoughts to become negative thoughts. And over time it affected the way I felt and eventually would begin to affect the way I acted. So much so that it seemed like my life was being surrounded by nothing but bad things and never any good, and this caused me to lose hope.

But when God removed my sin, which is represented as scales that were covering my spiritual eyes, blinding me to the ways of God. Little by little I began to see through both eyes again and saw my life becoming balanced. It became balanced because I was now able to see both truth and lies, and good and bad in all things, people and my circumstances. The whole picture and not just a small portion of it, and this allowed me the ability to make discernment between the two and made it easier to make the right choices. In other words, we are able to see more clearly the puzzle pieces God has provided for us and see where they belong, and begin to put the puzzle together the way he intended. And this makes the life that God hoped we would have possible.

He showed me that the puzzle in itself does represent our life and the things we will experience, but it is the order in which the puzzle pieces is put together that makes all the difference and makes the picture come to life in a way that we want and God wanted for us. Once we begin to live life in the order that God created it to work, then we see everything else fall into place. Things like receiving the wisdom and knowledge of him, which gives us the truth that will bring answers to our unanswered questions. And with answers you then have understanding, and this gives you the ability to let go, cleaning out the clutter in your mind that has caused you to fall into the spiritual valleys. With no more clutter to carry around, we are then able to forgive those who have hurt us because we have nothing there to remind us of what they did. And where there is forgiveness, we find freedom, and then we see our heart that once was hardened being filled with love and compassion. And this in turn gives us the ability to obey God in the way he commands us to do, which will bring blessings instead of the curses the Bible talks about. And it is his blessings that will give us the life on the mountaintop. But before we can begin to live our life in the order that God created it to be so all these things can take place, we first have to accept Jesus as Lord. From the beginning of time, our life experiences show us and God that we cannot work the puzzle alone because sin in us blinds us. That is why the Bible tells us in Romans 3:23, "For all have sinned and fall short of the glory of God." And in Romans 6:23, "The wages of sin is death." But in Romans 5:8 we are told, "But God demonstrates his own love for us in this; While we were still sinners, Christ died for us." In other words, because of the love that God has for all of us, he gave up his one and only Son to die for us so that we could be forgiven of our sins and become God's children and he could help us work the puzzle that he created for us and live the life that he intended for us to have. Only through Jesus do we find forgiveness and live, and when he rescues us, it causes us to want to rescue others we see who are in danger both in the physical and spiritual sense, and this allows God's glory to be revealed for all to see. This causes the puzzle to be completed because no longer are we (God and us) in two different places, working against one another, but we are both on the mountaintop together at the same time.

By allowing me to experience all that I did, he helped me see that I did need him, and this led me to accepting Jesus as my Lord, turning every area of my life over to him. This then allowed God to place me on that highway I saw in the vision that is called the Way of Holiness where life can be found. This made the puzzle God created for me possible. When he asked me to tithe, he positioned me to where I could receive his blessings, and this showed me how to work the puzzle in the order it was created to be worked. You first have to give to receive is what Luke 6:37–38 tells us. For it says, "Forgive, and you will be forgiven. Give and it will be given to you." When he asked me to read the Bible, he was presenting the puzzle and all of its pieces to me, allowing me the privilege of helping put it together, giving me back the control over what happens in my life. You could say it is our instruction book for life. When he showed me the vision, he was showing me the picture of the puzzle before I completed it so I would know what to expect and have the hope that I needed so I could have perseverance and endure the things I would experience in this world. When he asked me to go to church, he was helping me to work the puzzle, fulfilling his promise that he would never leave me nor forsake me (Hebrews 13:5). He was making sure that there would be no more mistakes made so that his plan and purpose for me could be fulfilled. God created the solution to my problems, but it was up to me to do all that he said to do so I could experience the results.

I know some may never be able to have this type of life in the here and now, even some who have been saved, because many are not willing to do what is needed to have it. But the picture and desire that

God has placed in us to have never goes away. And the reason is because his love for us never ceases to exist; neither does the hope he has for all of us. It is that hope that motivates one to keep trying when everything is telling you to quit. That is the reason God has never given up on us and continues to try new ways to help us see. When we cannot see or feel any hope, that is when we become afraid, and the fear will stop us in our tracks. Without hope we become dead inside, just like one who goes to the grave, as David said in Psalms 28:1. David realized, and I have come to realize, that God is our hope, and when we do not see or hear him, then the things we will experience will eventually cause us to feel as though life is not worth living.

With this new revelation, I began to realize that I had no control over what other people did, and I couldn't do anything to change the past, but I could do something to ensure my future with God's help. Because I realized it was my responsibility to find out what and how God says we are to live and then choose whether or not to do things his way or continue to do it the way the world does. And that is when I saw a really big change take place in me and my way of thinking and in my life. As far as my finances goes, he helped me see that yes for years even though I believed and I spoke this truth, I continued to look at my finances the way the world looks at them, and I was acting accordingly. I was the one trying to turn that curve on my own instead of trusting God to make it happen. And in the process I kept trying to put the wrong piece of the puzzle in the wrong place. And this caused me to fall off the mountain each time God placed me there. I wasn't doing what the Bible says, and that is, "Do not be anxious about anything, but in everything, by prayer and petition, with thanksgiving, present your request to God" (Philippians 4:6). In other words, have faith and cast your cares, your worries, and concerns on the one, the Bible tells us in Ephesians 3:20, "can do immeasurably more than all we ask or imagine, according to his power that is at work in us." And then he tells us to trust him when he tells us in Matthew 6:24, "Therefore do not worry about tomorrow, for tomorrow will worry about itself, each day has enough trouble of its own."

God had to make the picture clear in my eyes so I would be able to share it with others. But since he has, my life has become so much easier and more enjoyable; I believe that I am now living on the mountaintop. No we are not out of debt, but I now have the hope that one day we may be. Because I know that it is God's will for us because through Jesus he has provided a way for us to be set free from anything that makes us feel as if we are a slave. And debt can definitely make you feel as if you are a slave to your debtors. But in 2 Corinthians 3:17, it tells us, "Now the Lord is the Spirit, and where the Spirit of the Lord is, there is freedom." And every day I see myself becoming and living as one who has been set free because I have the Spirit of one and only living God living inside me.

My testimony in this book shows that I am no different than anyone else. I live in this world the same as everyone, and like a lot of people, I found myself in a valley because of some of the things I experienced in my life, and I didn't know how or in what way to get out of it. In this world, and as my testimony shows, even after Jesus became my Lord, I still experienced the sorrow of losing a loved one, financial woes, and my ongoing health problems. I believe that God wanted me to share the vision because of his love for all of us, and what he did for me he wants to do for others. And through my testimony, others could see the works of his outstretched arm in my life and see that he is Lord and see that with him it is possible to come out of the valleys we have fallen into. In Exodus 6:6, it tells us that God revealed to Moses and the other Israelites that he was Lord by the works of his outstretched arm that delivered them from bondage in Egypt. And this testimony along with many others was placed in the Bible as examples to all of us to teach and to warn us as it tells us in 1 Corinthians 10:11. And through these examples of others we read about, we will find the ability to endure the things we experience in this world, and be encouraged so that we might have hope as we make our way in this life (Romans 15:4). But we are also told in Acts 1:8, "You shall be witnesses to Me in Jerusalem, and in all Judea and Samaria, and to the ends of the earth." And this leads me to believe that God wants to use us who the Lord has helped, to be a testimony as well. Because it is through our testimony today that the glory of God can continue to be seen by those who do not know him as of yet.

This chapter of my journey shows how God was working in me so that I could begin to return to the valley and share my testimony and the vision with others. So I close out this chapter by asking, "Do you have a testimony that you have not shared with someone else yet?" Your willingness to share your gifts and testimony will glorify God through Jesus Christ (1 Peter 4:11). And it could be the determining factor on whether someone else comes out of a valley and is set free, or continues to live as Satan's slave and falls deeper into one.

Paying It forward

When God opens our spiritual eyes, I believe that is when we begin to see supernatural things happening to us and in our life. For me I didn't see myself in heaven or anything like that. But what did happen changed my life forever. Not only did God allow me to see his love for me and show me that I was his child, in his arms, and gave me what I needed to live. But it was like he allowed me to see the vision through his eyes, and this helped me to understand it. When he connected it to Psalms 23, it was like he allowed me the opportunity to feel what he feels every time he looks down at us in this world. And I will say that the feelings of anger and the feelings of sadness I felt in that moment were so intense that it was almost more than I could bear. This experience helped me to have more love and compassion for others because not only did he allow me to feel what he feels but also he helped me to understand the reasons behind those feelings. Even though it angers God to see his children worshiping other gods, he has led me to believe that he understands why we all tend to do that, and that is because he sees what Satan is doing in us. Because when he looks down at us and this world, he sees time repeating itself, because he hears the many cries for help and deliverance from all the people. We have become a slave in this world just like in the days of old (Egypt), and the slave master over us is Satan (Pharaoh), controlling and manipulating each person into doing his bidding. And that is stealing, killing, and destroying other people and their hopes and dreams by the things we say and do. And the end result is the vicious cycle that has been going on from generation to generation, continues with each new generation, he sees more people crying out to him for help. Then he showed me that he felt the sadness because he does hear the cries of the people. And because of those cries, he provided a way for everyone to escape Satan's hold on us through Jesus. Setting us free from whatever bondage or sins that Satan is using to keep us as his slaves. And through Jesus, he has made it possible for us to have a life in the promised land in the land we live in today, as well as the land he has provided where we will spend eternity. But because of the sin in us and in this world, we have eyes but we cannot see, and we have ears but we cannot hear from God, so we continue to live as slaves. And there are so many that will never experience the fullness of his love and goodness in this life and the life to come.

THE VISION

This experience that God allowed me to have has been the driving force behind me that has kept me going when times were difficult, and when I felt overwhelmed at times by all that he was showing me. I can only speculate, but maybe that is the reason God allowed me to have this experience to begin with so that I wouldn't give up. I just know that because of these feelings I have felt an urgency to do what I felt God ask me to do, and that is share the vision with as many people as I possibly can. No the vision is nothing new that was only shown to me because God has showed me what it is talked about throughout the Bible and is meant for everyone. My testimony of it, I feel, is just another way God is trying to open the eyes and ears of his people so they can begin to enjoy their journey as they make their way home to him.

It is now time to share things about the vision that will show that it wasn't just meant for me but everyone. To begin this process, I will begin by sharing the first thing that God revealed to me about it. That is, the vision is a symbol of our life. The life we live here in this world and the life we will experience once Jesus becomes our Lord and Shepherd. I have said that when I first saw the vision I saw myself standing on a long narrow highway that seemed to lead me to nowhere. It was almost like I was entering what we call Death Valley, because as far as I could see on either side of the highway there was no sign of life anywhere. As God began to help me understand the vision, he allowed me to see that I saw it in this way in the beginning because he needed for me to see this world that we live in today as it really is. And what we can expect as we make our way through it. There is one important fact that I feel he wants us to understand, and that is this world is one big valley, and as long as we are in this valley, we will always experience the death of something. For example, people work for years at a job they plan to retire from, but in some cases, they may lose that job and have to start all over. We have times when money doesn't seem to be an issue and other times when we struggle just to get by. We see people getting married, thinking they will spend all their life with that person that they love, but some do end up getting a divorce. And yes in this world we experience the death of loved ones, and even our own. That is the reason all the land looked so barren to me. God wants us to see that this world and the things in it represent death. That is the reason he does not want us to put our trust in man or the things of this world, because the things of this world will be with us one day and gone tomorrow and no one knows when that will happen.

As I looked down that long narrow highway, it looked to me as though it was going to disappear into the sky. The reason I saw it in this way was because God wants to give us hope for a better place than we live in today, a place where we can spend eternity, our home, when our work here on earth is done. And it is a place where we as believers know we will not have to fear the death of anything. For believers, knowing that this place is waiting for us is what will help us to endure the things we will encounter as we make our way through this valley. Because we know that death,

THE VISION

which is our ultimate fear, has no hold on us. There is life after this life.

The curve represents the mountaintop, and a time in our life when both God and us will be there at the same time. Because that is when we begin to see our will and God's will for us coming together and will see our plans, hopes, and dreams being fulfilled. I say this because God allowed me to see that his plans for us are the same as we want for ourselves. We want a life that is good, and he wants a life that is good for us because of the love he has for us. It is those desires that God has put within us to have this life that motivates us to keep moving forward so in the end his will can be fulfilled in our life. So the second important fact that we need to understand is, God does want us to have life and have it more abundantly just as Jesus said he came to give us in John 10:10. It is when we begin to understand that God's will is the same as ours that we are able to see that he is for us and not against us and no longer will we fight against him. I have come to believe that the vision is important for everyone because the vision will give us hope for things not yet seen, because it represent what God has told us in the Bible he will do. God placed this hope in me when he told me, "When you turn that curve, you will be debt free." But it is each person's responsibility to figure out what it is you are hoping for and then find out what God says about it in his Word and choose to believe it by faith.

During the first few years after seeing the vision, I believed that on the day God helped me to turn the curve, that would be the day he would take me home to heaven to be with him. Because in the beginning of my journey, I could not see any way I would ever be able to be debt free in this world. But in time, he helped me to understand that turning the curve didn't just represent becoming debt free, but in fact it represents our coming out of the valley. The turning of the curve represents our testimony that Jesus is Lord and that we have to share with others so that God can help others to find hope and be encouraged as they make their way out as well. This is just one way God is able to use us to help and bless more of his children and spread the good news about his kingdom and let his glory shine for all to see. It is our testimony of what the Lord does in our life that allows us to experience a little taste of heaven right here on earth. It is through his faithfulness to do what he says he will do that we are able to feel his presence and experience his love, mercy, and grace. It was at this time in my journey that I began to see more clearly that the kingdom of heaven does come in two stages, and it was possible to live the life that we hope for in this world as well as in heaven. Because through the things I was seeing Jesus do in my life, I found myself feeling the contentment that is needed to live on the mountain. I was seeing more and more that all things were possible through him. So therefore I believe that anyone who has faith in Jesus will be able to experience the same as I did because God's love and hope is the same toward everyone he created. I now realize that the turning of the curve doesn't just mean going home but returning to the valley where others are hurting to share our testimony. This allows us to show that Jesus is Lord and can do all things.

THE VISION

I turn my focus back to the highway because that is what the vision is really all about. Without it nothing else matters, because the highway is what connects and makes everything else possible in the here and now and the future for each one of us. In the spirit God allowed me to see all of us who try to live our life in this world without him. And what I saw was people wandering aimlessly about, going here and there, trying anything and everything in search for what we have lost and need and want out of life but never finding it. And the reason is because I saw Satan there stealing, killing, and destroying our hopes and dreams in any way possible and using anyone connected to us. After seeing this, I began to understand why Matthew 9:36 refers to us the people as sheep and tells us, "They were harassed and helpless, like sheep without a shepherd." This is the reason Jesus was sent to be our Shepherd. But then God allowed me to see that because of his love and hope for all of us, he provided a way out for us by providing this highway, and only the redeemed are allowed to walk on it. He even named the highway and called it the "Way of Holiness" (Isaiah 35:8).

The highway God provided for the redeemed not only represents our way out of the valley but also it represents a time in our life where we will no longer walk alone, because we will have Jesus and the Holy Spirit of God as our companion, a Shepherd for eternity. In John 10:11, Jesus tells us that he is the Good Shepherd. It is during our time spent with Jesus traveling down that highway that we learn the truth about God and the things of him that will help us to grow up spiritually and learn how to share our testimony with others. And our life and our way of thinking goes from being unbalanced to balanced. And even though we will not see him as we see ourselves or others, we will know that he is there with us. Because we will see and experience his love through the work of his outstretched arm in our life, and we will come to know that he is Lord. Taking all that seems impossible for us and making it possible so that he can continue to glorify the Father. For Jesus tells us in John 14:13–14, "I will do whatever you ask in my name, so that the Son may bring glory to the Father. You may ask me for anything in my name, and I will do it." It is through the things we will see Jesus do in us and for us as we travel down that highway that will cause our will to become the same as God's will for us, and we will see our faith grow and we will become confident so we can say, "The Lord is my Shepherd; I shall not be in want" (Psalms 23:1). I know this to be true because God has showed me that when he appointed Jesus to be my Lord and Shepherd, he placed me in his arms to care for my every need until the day comes when Jesus can place me in the arms of my Heavenly Father. And this he will do for all who have been redeemed and have faith in him.

Once we have been placed on this highway by God through Jesus, then the highway represents and becomes our place of refuge, and we come to realize what it is we can expect from God by the things we will see him do there. We will continue to experience Satan's attacks because we still live in this world. And we may even feel at times as Paul describes in 2 Corinthians 4:8–9, hard-pressed on every side, but we will not be crushed, perplexed, but we will not be in despair, persecuted, but we will not be abandoned, struck down, but we will not be destroyed. As you can see with every attack, there is a promise, and it is these promises of God that I feel he wants us to focus on as we run our race and come to expect as we make our way to turning the curve. It is these promises that will help us to keep the right attitude about life and give us hope. It is the hope that will make us strong so that we can endure and overcome the attacks. It is when we know and can see what the end result of our attacks will be that we are able to find the peace and rest from all our worries, fears, and concerns that God wants us to have (Psalms 23:2).

And then he showed me that if we could see this highway on a map what we would see is this highway is the road, the way, that leads us through this world. And because it is our place of refuge, it allows us to experience the promised land in the land we live in today, the kingdom of heaven of the here and now. Because it is while we are on this road we will see what is impossible for man being made possible with God. This causes our dry and barren land to turn into green pastures and flowing rivers just as it says in Psalms 23:2. And this makes us feel as though we are living on the mountaintop and no longer will we walk aimlessly about in search for something that we have lost. But this highway is also the road that leads us to the promised land of the future, because while on it we are transformed and made to be holy just as God is holy little by little. Because Psalms 23:3 tells us, "He restores my soul. He guides me in paths of righteousness for his name sake."

When God showed me the vision the third time, he allowed me to see the highway through both my physical and spiritual eyes, and I was able to see it as he sees it, because the highway turned into the Lord's staff. He did that to confirm to me and all people that Jesus was indeed the Shepherd he had sent to take care of us and to make sure we would make our journey home to heaven. But he also did it to confirm that he had given Jesus all the power and authority to do all things in heaven and on earth (Matthew 28:18). Because the staff was a symbol of God's power and authority in the days of Moses, and by it he revealed to Moses and the Israelites that he was Lord and nothing was too hard for him just as he will do in our lives today (Exodus 6:3–6).

By allowing me to see that I was in the Lord's arms, the Lord who he had given all authority to do whatever was needed in my life, it was his way of comforting me and letting me know I did not have to walk in fear of the unknown any longer. Because Jesus came and lived as we live in this world. He knows all there is to know about this world and the things we will experience, so therefore he can and will have compassion toward and wants to help us. And the Bible tells us that he overcame this world, even death itself. I believe that God wants us to know that when we ask Jesus to be our Lord and he comes to live inside of us, we have someone with us that knows the way and is more powerful than anyone or anything we may encounter.

THE VISION

And the Bible confirms this when we read 1 John 4:4, "You, dear children, are from God and have overcome them, because the one who is in you is greater than the one who is in the world" (Psalms 23:4). It is the death of something that causes us to feel as though we are in the valley. But when we come to realize that Jesus, the one who conquered death, lives inside of us and brings all the power and authority that was given to him with him, it is then we can say, "Death has been swallowed up in victory. Where, O death, is your victory? Where, O death, is your sting?" (1 Corinthians 15:34–35). We can and will give God thanks because we are a child in the Lord's arms and he gives us the victory through our Lord Jesus Christ (1 Corinthians 15:37).

As God was completing my understanding of the vision, he allowed me to see the last two things that are the most important to all of us that it represents. First, being the highway is Jesus. That is the reason he tells us in John 14:6, "I am the way the truth and the life. No one comes to the Father except through me." It is only because of what Jesus did are we forgiven of our sins and made holy just as God is holy. And this causes us to become God's children, heirs of God and coheirs with Christ (Romans 8:13–14). It is by him that we are shown the way through this valley to the mountain. It is from him that we hear the truth that causes our lives to become balanced where we can discern between the truth from God and the lies of Satan and make the right choices in our life that will lead us to the mountaintop. Once the truth comes into our life, that is what starts the ball rolling that gives us everything else that is needed. Like the wisdom and knowledge we need that will give us the answers to all our whys, whats, hows, and whens that life throws at us and will set us free to live a life on the mountain. Because Jesus tells us in John 8:32, "Then you will know the truth, and the truth will set you free." It is the Word of God that will arm us so that we can be the conqueror rather than the conquered in this world. For it tells us in Ephesians 6 that the sword we need for battle is the Word of God. It is by Jesus's name God has given us power-of-attorney rights so that we as his children can do all that Jesus does and share in the promise that was made possible through the covenant God made with Abraham making us coheirs with Christ. For Jesus tells in John 14:12–13, "I tell you the truth, anyone who has faith in me will do what I have been doing. He will do even greater things than these, because I am going to the Father. And I will do whatever you ask in my name, so that the Son may bring glory to the Father." Through my own experiences, I have seen that Jesus is the Way the Truth and the Life and have seen for myself what God tells us in Colossians 3:4, "When Christ, who is your life, appears, then you also will appear with him in glory" (Psalms 23:5).

As I come to the end of sharing the vision and the connection it has with Psalms 23, I share the final revelation God gave me about it. The vision in a whole represents God's grace to all of us. In other words, it is the picture of life's puzzle God wants all of us to see. The vision was not only important for me but for everyone because it shows us that it is through his

Son, Jesus, God is able to reveal and mediate his grace toward all of us. Because of his grace, God allowed his Son to die so that we could live. It is through the grace of God that he made it possible for us to approach the throne of grace with confidence so that we may receive mercy and find grace to help us in our time of need (Hebrews 4:16). It is because of the grace of God we are able to see that we have all received one blessing after another (John 1:16). It is because of God's grace and his faithfulness to do what he says he will do that I and anyone else who will accept this grace can live, getting up every morning expecting to see goodness and love following us all the days of our life. I can say this because I have experienced God's grace in my life, and I know I have God with me and he is Love (1 John 4:8) and represents all that is good (1 Corinthians 13:4–7) And I know whatever is his is mine, and wherever he is, there I will be also, because he has shown me I am his child in his arms, making me his heir (Psalms 23:6).

I will be the first to say that when God showed me the vision and began to help me understand it, there were times when it seemed so complicated and complex that it was hard for my simple mind to understand it all. But I have to give God praise because he understood my struggles and had patience with me and worked through the things I experienced daily to help me understand and be able to do what he called me to do. From the beginning I have known in my heart that it wasn't just the vision I was supposed to share, but it had a message that come along with it. This is what I have had the most difficulty in wrapping my mind around and has taken the most time to bring about. Because even though I understood it in my heart, God was calling me to share it with others, and I didn't know how to do that.

It wasn't until we finished our discipleship training class that God was able to show me what it was he wanted me to pass on to others. The first being the vision of course, but also the answers to the questions we all seem to have. By having these questions answered, we will see more clearly the problem, the solution, and then know what needs to be done to get the results that we want and God wants for us. The first question we all seem to ask is, "Why is God allowing me to experience the valleys?" I believe we find the answer to this question in the same message we have all heard time and time again. John 3:16, "For God so loved the world that he gave his one and only Son, that whoever believes in him shall not perish but have eternal life." Romans 5:8, "But God demonstrates his own love for us in this; While we were still sinners Christ died for us." When God created the first man and woman because of his love for them, he created them to live a full and abundant life and provided all that they could ever want, need or desire. But as we see in the scriptures sin interfered with God's plan because it tells us in Romans 3:23, "For all have sinned and fall short of the glory of God." And the wages of sin is death (Romans 6:23). But because God is faithful to fulfill his plan for all of us and his love he has for us will never change, he gave up all that was important to him, and Christ died in our place because of our sins so that we could live and receive

God's promise of life. We see through what God has done that there was a plan for life when he created it, and how he created a solution to get rid of the sin in us that prevented his plan from ever being fulfilled as he intended. And his determination and faithfulness to see that those plans were fulfilled even if that meant his Son had to die to do it. Upon seeing this love he had for me and the extremes he went to, to ensure that we live and have life in heaven for eternity, I soon come to realize with God's help that this same love for us wanted us to live and have life in the promised land in the land we live in today. And I believe that is what God wanted me to share with others. It is our sin and disobedience that causes us to be separated from God and makes us feel as though we are living in the valleys, because it opens the door and allows Satan to come in and destroy us.

The next question we tend to ask is, "How do I come out of the valley?" The answer to this question will show us the solution to our problem. When we finished our class at the church, I heard some say that people needed to hear a quick and simple solution to their problems. And if they didn't, we would not be able to keep their attention long enough so that they could find the help they needed to come out of the valleys they had fallen into. It was because of this response that I found myself feeling as though I had failed God and the people who attended our class. Because I saw very quickly that they still did not understand. And then God begin to show me that this is the problem and has been the problem for some time. It is because we live in this fast-paced, sinful world with all its difficulties, and we are all looking for quick and simple solutions so that we don't have more added to our to-do lists. But in the process of looking for those quick and simple solutions, we have failed to see that because God does hear the cries of the people for help and he wants to dry ever tear because of his love for us, he provided our quick and simple solution to all of our problems by sending us Jesus.

Once while the Lord was speaking to me, he said, "Many people come to me and ask for forgiveness of their sins and promise me that they will allow Jesus to be their Lord. And I am faithful to do what I said I would do. I forgive them of their sins, I write their name in the book of life and I make ready a place in heaven for them where they can spend eternity with me just as I promised. But before most get up from their knees, they begin to take back the promise they made me, because they go back to being lord over their lives. And this is what saddens me because when this happens, they are not able to experience the fullness of my love and goodness in this life. It is there for their taking through Jesus, yet they choose not to receive it."

I am led to believe that what God wanted me to share is that he takes our promises, the covenant agreement we have made with him, very seriously. And for us to live a life in the promised land we live in today, our relationship with him cannot be one-sided. Our life in heaven was a gift from God to all of us who believe and proof of God's love for us. But to have the life we want and God wants for us in the here and now, we will be required to fulfill our part in the covenant agreement so that we can show proof of our love for him. And this means we will be required to do something that involves having faith in Jesus and allowing him to be Lord over our lives. This world we live in is not perfect in the way heaven will be for us, so it takes cooperation on both parties so that we can see happen what we want and God wants for us. Without both parties doing what is required the covenant promises that God put in place through Jesus to help us in this world cannot be seen in our life today. There will be times as the Lord leads you down that highway you will be the one to receive something given because those are the times when you will see God's love and grace doing for you. But then there will be other times you will have to be the giver of something received. That is when you will see God asking you to do something for him. This relationship with the Lord is sort of like what we see happening in a marriage between a husband and a wife and what happened in my life as God led me down that highway. It is a relationship that requires both parties' willingness to give as well as take to make it work.

The questions I have been led by the Lord to ask is this, "After all that you have read, heard, and seen that Jesus can and will do, why will you not allow him to be Lord and allow him to do what I sent him to do for you? Do you still have no faith?" I have been led by the Lord to believe that these questions are meant for everyone, especially those who are struggling with life in this world. God had been asking me these same questions for years over and over, and I found that giving an answer wasn't that easy. Maybe that is the reason I ran away from him in the past. It wasn't until I began to do a lot of soul-searching and asked myself other questions first was I able to answer God's questions.

These are just some of the questions I had to ask myself.

1. What is it that I am looking for that would make me feel as if I was living on the mountaintop?

I found this to be a very important question because you have to know what it is exactly that you are looking for; otherwise, you will not know when you have found it. As you ask this question, remember that if your answer consists of mainly material things, the material things represent this world and will eventually need to be replaced. And when this happens, you could find yourself back in a valley.

2. Has what I have been doing up to this point allowed me to find what I am looking for? If so, for how long?

When answering this question, you are looking for consistency, something that does not cause you to feel up one minute and down the next. If you see that your answer to this question is no, then you have to ask yourself why.

It was while I was asking myself why and reflecting back on my life that I realized that nothing I had done or could do was going to make a difference in my life because I had spent forty years trying and had failed. And that is when I had to ask myself these questions.

3. Are you so tired of living in the valley and being miserable that you are willing to do something about it, even if it means it could be difficult for you at times?
4. Can it be any worse trying to do things God's way?
5. Is there a possibility it could be better? What do you have to lose?

Yes, I came to the Lord because I didn't know what else to do and was desperate. Because at the time even though dying seemed to be easier than living, the truth of the matter was I really didn't want to die at all. I just wanted things to change and the hurting to stop. Afterward, when some of the burdens had been lifted, that is when I had to ask myself these questions along with many others. It was these questions I was asking myself that helped me see that love is what I was in need of to make me happy. After thinking about this for a while, I was able to see that we were created by the one who is Love, to be loved, and to show our love to others. Without love we live feeling as though something is missing in our life, because love brings to us a reason to exist. I couldn't find the love I needed to make me feel whole and complete in other people or the things in this world because the things of this world can't give love. And all the people I was turning to couldn't give it in the way I needed because they were searching for it as well. But when I accepted Jesus as my Lord and my Shepherd and turned everything over to him, God allowed me to live out the vision and see for myself that he is the true unconditional love that we all need and are all looking for to live, and through Jesus he is able to mediate his love for us to us. This is why I believe God wanted me to share that Jesus is our quick and simple solution to whatever problems we may encounter in our life. As long as we are able to love others the way God calls us to love and we are able to receive love from others in the way God wants us to, we can get through whatever we may encounter because love will never fail to do what is right or what is good. And good is what the mountaintop represents. So the last and final question that you will need to ask yourself is,

> 6. Will you allow Jesus to be your Lord and Shepherd, and allow God to show you that Jesus is your quick and simple solution because of his love he has for you?

Maybe you have never prayed the prayer of salvation, or maybe you have but have not yet turned every area of your life over to Jesus and allowed him to be Lord. Either way if your answer is yes to question 6. Jesus is waiting to see you open the door to your life and allow him to come in. For he tells us in Revelation 3: 20, "Here I am! I stand at the door and knock. If anyone hears my voice and opens the door, I will come in and eat with him, and he with me." And I know from my own experience that if you let him in, he will pick you up in his arms and carry you down that highway and will never let you go. And no matter what happens along the way, you will be okay because he will see you through it. For it tells us in Isaiah 43:2–3, "When you pass through the waters, I will be with you; and when you pass through the rivers, they will not sweep over you. When you walk through the fire, you will not be burned; the flames will not set you ablaze. For I am the Lord, your God, the Holy One of Israel, your savior."

It was when we were coming to the end of our discipleship training class that God began to wrap things up and showed me the last bit of information he wanted me to share. The last question I believe we are looking for the answer to is, "When can I expect to see myself coming out of the valley?" The only way I know how to relay that is by referring back to my own testimony and what God did with me. He first had to get me to come to him and he did that by using my past experiences to show me that I needed him. The question you will need to ask yourself is, "How long are you willing to wait before you come to Jesus and follow him?" Once I come to him, he then asked me to go and do. He showed me that he is the creator of the mountain we are all striving to get to, both in the here and now and the future. So for us to achieve a life on the mountain, we have to be willing to come to the one that provides it when he says, "Come follow me," becoming humble before the Lord. Our willingness to come will allow us to experience the kingdom of heaven in the future, God's gift to all of us. But to experience the kingdom of heaven in the here and now, God will ask us to go and do just as he asked me, which means we will have to walk by faith and trust him as he leads us down that highway that leads to the mountaintop. Submit to doing his will and not our own and obey in what he tells us to do. This means you will have to ask yourself, "Am I willing to go and do whatever he ask of me, allowing him to be Lord?" And last and most important we have to be willing to allow him to show us how to be content in all things. These are the five steps that the Lord helped me to take that led me out of the valley and placed me on the mountain, and I have been led by the Lord to share so others who are willing to follow these steps can find the mountaintop as well as he helps them along. Hopefully all who are reading this will see that you have been given the power to determine if you will continue to live in the valleys, and when you will come out, because God has given you the freedom to choose what you want.

In the midst of helping me to take these five steps, there were four things he asked me to do and places he asked me to go. But no one can say for sure if the Lord will ask others to do what he asked of me or in that order because we are all different with different needs. But there is one thing you can be sure of. When you enter into a relationship with the Lord, you will be asked to do something or go somewhere so that his love for you and your love for him may be shown for all to see and he is able to help you with whatever you are in need of. I understand that he asked me to tithe because tithing positioned me to be able to receive from God. Since money is what I was in need of to get out of debt, I had to be willing to give money to receive the money needed to do what God asked me to do. Reading the Bible allowed me to get to know God, because he is the Word, so I would know what I could expect from him and what he wanted from me and the covenant agreement between the two of us could be fulfilled. I know my willingness to read the Bible is what transformed me and made me a new creation. By reading and having God's Word inside me, it got rid of the clutter in my mind, changed my way of thinking, and taught me how to forgive those who had hurt me and set me free, and this allowed me to let go of my past, which brought healing to the wounds my past had created. Going to church helped me to be around other people who were God's children already and learn from their example and receive the help I was in need of. I was able to hear the Word that developed my faith even more and taught me how to obey. Without obedience, Jesus cannot be Lord in our life. And finally it helped me to grow up spiritually and learn how to be content in all things, because without contentment we cannot have the life on the mountaintop. We will always be searching for something else, and that will lead us back to the valley.

My testimony is one example of what happens when we try to live our life without God being a part of it. But it is also one example of what can happen when we choose Jesus to be our Lord. What I have been led by the Lord to share with others is, because of his love for us he wants his children to know that life is possible in the here and now. But only if we are first willing to allow Jesus to take hold of our hand and lead us down that highway. This means we have to choose to be patient and wait as the Lord works to remove the scales from your spiritual eyes so that we can see to make our way. Allow him the time to develop your faith and trust in him as he works, even when you don't understand what he is doing. Doing his will, even if what he is asking you to do will go against what the flesh wants you to do or what comes natural to you. Obeying him even in those times when it would be so easy or more gratifying to disobey. These things don't come naturally to us, and yes, at times it may be very difficult for us. But because of my experience I can now say that when we are willing to work together with Jesus, it is then that all these things I have mentioned becomes possible and begins to bring us out of the valleys. It is our faithfulness to Jesus working along with his faithfulness to the Father that will allow us to become content and place us on the mountaintop.

As for me, I do believe the Lord wants to prosper us in every area of our life. So therefore, I believe that I will turn that curve and become debt free in this world. Because just as it tells us in John 8:36, "If the Son makes you free, you shall be free indeed." And I know that God always finishes what he starts. Because he tells us in Isaiah 46:11, "What I have said, that I will bring about; What I have planned, that will I do." And because he has told me that Jesus paid all my debts in full, I will now wait and enjoy the anticipation of things not yet seen. And whether I see it happen while I am among the living or by him taking me home to be with him, it doesn't really matter to me any longer because I know either way I am blessed because I am with him and he is with me. And I will sing his praises, giving him all honor and all the glory because he has helped me turn that curve in more ways than I can count. But in the meantime, I will continue to say with confidence, expectation, and an overflowing of joy in my heart Psalms 23.

1. The Lord is my Shepherd; I shall not be in want.
2. He makes me lie down in green pastures, he leads me beside quiet water,
3. He restores my soul. He guides me in paths of righteousness for his name sake.
4. Even though I walk through the valley of the shadow of death, I will fear no evil, for you are with me; your rod and your staff they comfort me.
5. You prepare a table before me in the presence of my enemies. You anoint my head with oil; my cup overflows.
6. Surely goodness and love will follow me all the days of my life, and I will dwell in the house of the Lord forever.

I will say, now and for eternity, worthy is the lamb that was slain, that become my Shepherd who leads me, and deserves all honor and glory and my praise. Amen!

I know everyone has a journey to travel, and I know that the roads that the Lord has chosen for each person will be different, but it will be designed to meet their needs. But I also know he has provided this highway for anyone who will claim it as their own. And he has a hope of a destination that will be the same for all who confesses him as Lord. And that is a life on his mountain both in the here and now and the future. Because God has showed me through the vision and the things I have seen him do in my life that wherever he is the kingdom of heaven can be found also an his love for us will do more for us than we could ever imagine. But it is our chose on whether we will ever experience it.

So as I close out this chapter of my journey, I challenge anyone who is reading this book to not just take my word for it but take the time to investigate for yourself and find out if what I have said is not true. For Jesus said in Matthew 7:7–8, "Ask and it will be given to you; seek and you will find; knock and the door will be opened to you. For everyone who asks receives; he who seeks finds; and to him who knocks the door will be opened." My prayer is that no matter where you are at in your journey, and if you have found yourself in a valley and in need of help, you will come to know the love of Christ our Lord, for he is only a prayer away. And one day when our work is done here on earth, we will all stand together encircled around the throne, along with the angels the living creatures and the elders and sing in a loud voice,

> "Worthy is the lamb, who was slain.
> To receive power and wealth and wisdom and
> Strength and honor and glory and praise!"
>
> Revelation 5:11–12

November 14, 2013
Barbara Wilkes

About the Author

Who Is B SW?

My name is Barbara Sue (Horton) Wilkes, born in Tulsa, Oklahoma, on October 21, 1956. I am the oldest of three children, a sister of Rebecca Lynn and Lonnie Dwayne Horton. Our parents were Johnny and Geneva Sue Horton of Crowder, Oklahoma.

Even though my parents lived in Tulsa when I was born, they would move back to the rural town of Crowder where they grew up, shortly after. And there I would spend the first thirteen years of my life being surrounded by grandparents, aunts and uncles, cousins, nieces and nephews. At the age of twelve years old, my parents would get a divorce because my father had been molesting me since I was four years old and it had become known. A year later, my mother would remarry and become Mrs. Carl Hoffman. This man would be the man my sister, brother, and I call Dad today and our children call Grandpa. We moved back to Tulsa at that time, and it would be the place we would come to call home.

It would be there I would attend school and graduate in 1974 from Rogers High School. But in 1972, just a couple of years before I was to graduate, I was introduced to a young man that I couldn't seem to keep my eyes off of. And on September 14, 1973, this young handsome man Freddy Wilkes would become my husband, and we would start a new life together. Neither one of us came from a family of money, so our new adventure together was nothing extravagant but simple. Instead of spending our money on a honeymoon, we took it and got us a place to live. After four years of marriage, we bought our first home and decided to start a family. On August 12, 1978, our daughter, Melissa, was born.

My husband Freddy came from a very large family. He was one of eleven children. So at the age of fifteen, he dropped out of school and went to work as a carpet installer, which he still is today. I was a wife and mother first and only worked outside the home whenever his work was slow. I grew up kind of a loner, so the jobs I took never seemed to keep my interest for very long. Whenever Freddy's work would pick back up, I would quit and find contentment in taking care of the house and spending time with our daughter. The jobs I did have that lasted for any amount of time were entrepreneur-type jobs, jobs I could do from home. But in 1995, I would go into partnership with a friend of mine, and we would open a child care center we would call Happy Beginnings. But a year after we opened, she decided this wasn't what she wanted to do, so I became sole owner.

During the ten years of operating my own business, Freddy and I watched our daughter get married, and we became proud grandparents of twin girls Mikayla and Marissa. They were born on May 25, 1999. Freddy and I were no different from most. We enjoyed the joys and struggles of everyday life together. But for me there seemed to be something missing. For so many years, I had got stuck in my past because of the abuse, being blinded to the opportunities of joy, peace of mind, and true happiness. But then ten years ago, I realized I needed help. I realized I needed the Lord. What a difference that decision made in my life. Today I can tell you, I am fifty-four years old and happier than I have ever been. Even though life continues to go on with all its ups and downs, I can enjoy a sense of peace I have never felt before. With God's help, I can now say my past has been laid to rest and can no longer torment me in my future. Freddy and I will be celebrating our thirty-eighth anniversary this year as man and wife. And I now know who I am supposed to be and have found the peace, joy, and happiness I searched for, for so many years. God is now leading me on a new adventure of writing. And just as he has used it to bring new hope of better days to come in my life, hopefully he will be able to use it to bring new hope of better days to come in the lives of the people who read it.